This Teacher's Guide was designed for teachers of Pre-adolescent Children (9 to 11 years old)

TEACHER'S GUIDE
YEAR 2

I0157270

Corresponds to Year 2 of the cycle of three years of WORDS OF LIFE (Pre-adolescent Children) Teacher's Guides.

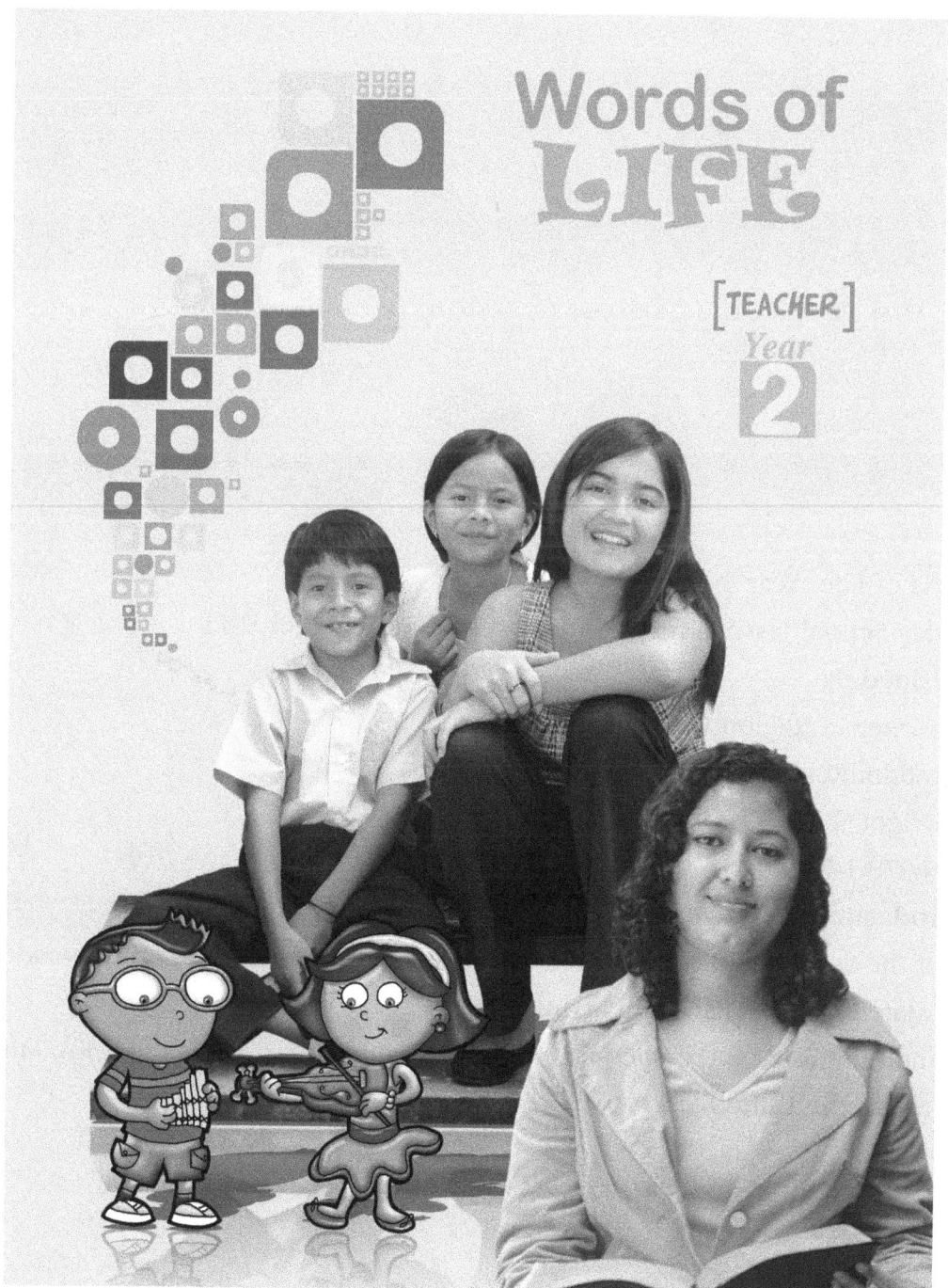

WORDS OF LIFE

Words of LIFE

[TEACHER]
Year
2

Words of Life, Year 2 - Teacher's Guide

Sunday School lessons for Pre-adolescent Children ages 9-11

Published by:

Mesoamerica Region Discipleship Ministries

www.SdmiResources.MesoamericaRegion.org

Copyright © 2018 - All rights reserved

ISBN:978-1-63580-115-6

All of the scripture verses quoted are from the NIV Bible unless otherwise noted.

Translated into English from Spanish by:

Amanda Englishbee (Lessons 1-10), Emily Raquel Gularte Oliva (11-30), Monte Cyr (31-52)

Printed in the United States

Mesoamerica Region

Table of Contents

HELPS FOR THE TEACHER

I. GENERAL ASPECTS OF THE LESSON AND THE UNIT

INTRODUCTION TO EACH UNIT

In it you will find the biblical basis for the whole unit, the biblical text, the purpose, the titles of the lessons and the reasons why the students need the teaching of this unit.

EACH LESSON CONTAINS:

Biblical References

Points out the biblical passage from which the lesson was taken. It can refer to one or more books or passages of the Bible. You must read the passage(s) and become familiar with them.

Lesson Objective

It clarifies where you should go with your students and what you should achieve through the teaching and learning process.

Memory Verse

It is considered more appropriate to use a single bible verse for the whole unit, with the purpose of emphasizing the central truth.

II. PREPARE YOURSELF TO TEACH!

PREPARE YOURSELF TO TEACH! and Biblical commentary

This second section presents a help for the biblical study passage, which will expand your knowledge on the subject. It also includes a biblical context and the way in which children of this age learn. For greater effectiveness, take into account the following:

- Pray and ask for God's direction.
- Read the Bible passage several times and write down in a notebook the central ideas you find.
- Consult other versions of the Bible, biblical commentaries, biblical dictionaries, etc.
- Compare your ideas with those presented in this book.
- Meditate on each of them, and reflect on how the passage applies to your own life and the lives of your students.

III. DEVELOPMENT OF THE LESSON

Here the different points of the lesson's development are identified. The Bible story must be presented with methods in which your students are actively participating. Be sure that the key points are clear in the minds of the children. You can practice the presentation of the theme in your home to be at ease in front of the students. Cheer up! The work is of the Lord, and you are an instrument in His hands to carry it out.

Bible story and Application for life

This is the moment for the student to reflect on his daily life. It is time to guide him to ask how his life is compared to what the Bible teaches. In general, these are activities with questions to answer in a personal way. Direct the preadolescent towards reflection and do not manipulate their answers, since these must be sincere and personal.

IV. ACTIVITIES

a. In this section you will find another series of reinforcement activities for the lesson, such as tasks in the activity sheets and games.
b. Memorization of the text, games.
c. To Finish: moments of prayer and reflection.

Suggestions:

- Keep in mind that it is best to prepare your lesson throughout the week, giving God's Holy Spirit opportunities to teach you, give you illustrations for the lesson, etc.
- Visit your students at least once every semester.
- Pray and communicate with students through letters, texts, phone calls, invitations, etc. Be sure to quickly contact them/visit them if they stop attending the class.
- Send a note to the student and / or parents and mention special facts in the student's life, such as birthdays, special days, etc.

- Encourage your students through contests to motivate them to attend, learn, memorize texts, invite their friends, etc.
- Arrive early to be sure you have the room ready for the class.
- When preparing lessons, take into account the age, needs and problems of preadolescents.
- As the teacher, you are also a friend, counselor and Christian model worth imitating.

SUGGESTIONS FOR BIBLE MEMORIZATION

1. WHAT DOES THE VERSE SAY?

Have your students express what the verse says by using their senses.

See
- In the Bible.
- Visual Aids: on the chalk/white board, signs, posters, flashcards, etc.

Hear
- Read it out loud
- Record it and play it back

Speak
- Repeat it after listening to it
- Read it together and individually
- Sing it

Touch
- Write the verse.
- Fill in the blank.
- Solve a crossword
- Use hand motions

2. WHAT DOES IT MEAN?

Explore the definitions.
- Let the kids express what they understand about each Bible verse.
- Explain words they don't understand.

Discuss the context.
- For more explanation, use Bible commentaries, dictionaries and other resources.
- Investigate the background of the verse.
- Who is speaking and to whom are they speaking?

Illustrate it.
- Show pictures/illustrations of the text.
- Create your own drawings.
- Use hand motions, sign language or act it out.

3. HOW DO I APPLY IT TO MY LIFE?

Discuss the following:
- The daily life application of this verse.
- In which circumstances will it be useful and what effect will it have on your life and others' lives.

Remember a Bible verse:
- When you are being tempted.
- When you are troubled.
- When you want to encourage others.

The Students, Their Behavior And The Teacher

1. Understand Your Students and Allow For Normal Behavior.

- Children are active and curious.
- They are not miniature adults: we must always differentiate between bad behavior and immaturity.

2. Create An Atmosphere That Promotes Good Behavior.

- Let children know that you love them and appreciate them.
- Show interest in what happens to them outside of class.
- Be organized in how you handle the students.
- Provide clear and consistent guidelines; let the children know what you expect of them.
- Don't show favoritism.

3. Acknowledge Your Position As A Teacher.

- Be in charge of the class.
- Be a figure of authority that students can follow.
- Become a friend to your students.
- Explain to them what is expected of them and give them good examples.

4. Use Methods That Involve the Children and Capture Their Interest.

- Be prepared and get to the classroom before any of the children.
- Provide a variety of activities that are appropriate for your students' ages.
- Use activities that capture their interest and ability.
- Allow children to choose some of the activities.

5. Focus on Positive Behavior.

- Limit the number of rules.
- When you correct a child, discuss it with their parent, guardian, or the person responsible for them.

WHAT DO YOU DO WHEN A CHILD MISBEHAVES?

1. Find the Cause of the Problem.

- Does the child have learning or medical problems that prevent their participation in class?
- Does he try to control the class?
- Is he academically talented and therefore bored with the class?
- When you know the cause of the problem, you may be able to correct it after talking with the child's parents.

2. Take Control of the Situation.

- Ignore behavior that doesn't interrupt the class.
- Include the child in learning activities.
- Let him see that you are observing his misconduct.
- Approach the child in a loving manner.
- Tell the child, quietly, what you want him to do.
- Teach students the consequences of continued misconduct.

3. Talk to Parents or the Person Responsible for the Child.

- If you know that you will most likely have to talk to his parents or guardian, do it.
- Start by telling the parents what you appreciate about their child.
- State the problem and ask for their ideas of how to resolve the problem..

LET'S MEET THE PRE-ADOLESCENT

This is an age of discovery.

> » They want to express their ideas.
> » They are physically and mentally "mature" enough.
> » They enjoy doing new activities.
> » They enjoy discussions that require complete answers.
> » They don't like "yes" and "no" answers anymore.
> » They enjoy working as a team.
> » They enjoy listening to stories, especially stories about Jesus.

As a teacher, encourage them to daily discover their life in Christ. Challenge them to do God's will.

When considering the characteristics of the development stage of your students, we include some tips to improve the dynamics of your class:

- Inspire your students with the stories of heroes of the Bible.
- Take the opportunity to teach them to memorize the Word, songs, and inspiring stories.
- Ask for the preadolescent's participation in the search of biblical passages, preparation for the classes, telling the Bible stories, doing dramas, looking for maps, doing puzzles, writing on the board or making posters about the lesson.
- Encourage them to participate with questions and answers to their classmates.
- Encourage them to imitate the biblical characters.
- It is an excellent time for them to form good habits such as: daily reading of the Bible, prayer, attending church, giving their tithes, talking to others about Jesus.
- Offer opportunities for students of this age to help others.
- Take this time to accept Jesus as their personal savior.
- Do extracurricular activities, lessons are not only taught or learned in the classroom. Always ask for the help of other adults.

TEACHING RESOURCES: RECIPES

Recipes for Play Dough or Molding Clay

Flour and Salt Dough

Ingredients:
2 or 3 Cups of Flour
¾ Cup Fine Salt
½ Cup Warm Water
Food Coloring

Instructions:
Mix the flour with the salt and add the warm water little by little as you stir. If you want it to be colorful, add drops of food coloring as it thickens. The consistency of the dough will depend on the amount of water you add. Store in a closed container in the fridge.

Cooked Dough

Ingredients:
2 Cups of Flour
1Cup Salt
1 Tablespoon Vegetable Oil
2 Teaspoons
Food Coloring

Instructions:
Mix the dry ingredients and then add the water and the vegetable oil. Cook the mix over low heat until it thickens, stirring it constantly. Take it away from the heat and let it cool. To make it the color you want, add drops of food coloring while you mix the dough. If kept in a closed container, it should last for over a month.

Mud Dough

Ingredients:
2 Cups of Dirt
2 Cups of Sand
½ Cup of Salt
Water

Instructions :
Mix the dirt, sand, and salt, and then add water a little at a time until you get a consistency that is good for molding.

Finger Paint

Ingredients:
1 ¼ Cup Corn Starch
½ Cup Powdered Soap
3 Cups Boiling Water
1 Tablespoon Glycerin
Food Coloring

Instructions:
Dissolve the starch in cold water. Pour it into the warm water slowly as you stir to avoid clumps. Add the soap and the glycerin. To add color, use food coloring. This recipe is not toxic. If stored in plastic cups, it should last several days.

White Glue

Ingredients:
4 Cups Water
1 Cup Wheat Flour
½ Cup Sugar
½ Cup Vinegar

Instructions:
Boil 3 cups of water. Meanwhile, in a container, mix one cup of water, flour, sugar, and vinegar. When the water starts to boil, add the mix and stir slowly over the heat. If there are clumps, stir it more. If it's too thick, add water. If it's too thin, boil it for longer. Store in a jar with a lid.

PAPER FOR CARDS AND CRAFTS

1. Soak 6 sheets of paper or pages from a magazine torn into small pieces in hot water.
2. Put it in the blender with half a cup of oatmeal or flowers or vegetables such as carrots or celery.
3. Strain the mixture and add 4 tablespoons of glycerin and 6 tablespoons white glue.
4. Spread the paste on a plastic sheet/tray with a rolling pin or stick until thin and even.
5. Let it dry in the sun for two days.
6. You can use this paper to make cards, bookmarks, letters, etc.

THE IMPORTANCE OF PROMOTING STUDENTS TO THE NEXT CLASS

Dear leaders and teachers of Sunday School and Christian education:

As is done for school, it is important for the children of the church to be promoted to the next class each year. As a teacher, it is very important that you are prepared to promote your students at the end of the course, which would be easiest at the end of the school year.

You may prepare a ceremony beforehand and give a certificate to the students who are moving on to the next class. The ceremony can be held at the church so the whole congregation may participate. Invite the parents and family members of the students. It would be a good time to get to know them and for them to attend the remainder of the service and listen to God's Word.

The teachers of the classes to which the students will be promoted should be present as special participants. It will be a significant moment for everyone when you as the teacher send the students to the next class with a hug, and the next teacher receives them likewise with a welcome embrace.

It would be nice if you had a poster with pictures of the students taken throughout the years they spent in your class. It would also be nice to share memories of the students while they were in your class: special prayers they said, the date they accepted Christ, stories they shared, questions they asked, and moments of joy or sadness they went through while in your class. Explain this to your students so they can agree with what you will share about them. This way they do not get embarrassed in front of the whole congregation.

Speak to the person in charge of Christian education or of the classes, so that at the ceremony, new books or Bibles can be given to the students for the following year. Encourage families from the church to gift a book to each student, especially to the ones whose parents do not attend the church or to the ones with financial struggles. In each congregation there are families that would gladly gift books to the students.

We wish you blessings in the challenges that the ministry of teaching presents for you and your congregation.

May the Lord give you grace and bless your important ministry.

Editorial Team

Certificate of Promotion

_____
(Student's name)

is promoted to the _____ _class_

_____
Church

_____
Date

"My child, pay attention to what I say…" Proverbs 4:20a

_____
Sunday School Superintendent

_____
Teacher

TO LIVE BETTER

Biblical References: Genesis 1:27-31; 2:1-3; Exodus 19:1-20:21; Psalms 119:9; Proverbs 12:22; Matthew 5:17, 21-22, 27-28, 33-37, 6:19-21; 24-31; 12:1-13, 35-37; Mark 12:28-34; Acts 5:1-10; Ephesians:4:25-26, 28-29; 5:3-4; 6:1-3; Philippians 4:10-13; 19; Colossians 3:8-9; James 1:19-20; Hebrews 13:5

Unit Text: "Love the Lord your God with all your heart and with all your soul and with all your mind and with all your strength. The second is this: 'Love your neighbor as yourself.'" (Mark 12:30-31a)

Unit Purposes: This unit is to help students to:

- Know that God gave his people the Ten Commandments to guide them to a Holy life.
- Learn that loving God and others are important commandments.
- To show Christian love in their interpersonal relationships.
- Recognize that God's guidance is important in order to live correctly.

Unit Lessons:

Lesson 1 – First things First

Lesson 2 – Power of Words

Lesson 3 – A special day

Lesson 4 – We need our parents

Lesson 5 – What do you see?

Lesson 6 – I Am Special

Lesson 7 – If it's not yours, leave it alone.

Lesson 8 – Lying brings consequences

Lesson 9 – Don't envy

Why do children need to learn this unit?

Due to the lose of values in our current world, we find ourselves living in a spiritually poor place. In addition, there are many ways to live your life that are taught, many of them being dangerous and not of God.

Your students are constantly bombarded with messages that show disobedience and anarchy as enticing things. It gets harder and harder to control student's reactions to what they see. Frequently, we hear that the police have had to come and intervene at schools due to student riots and violent acts.

We all need to know that God left firm instructions for his children to life a Holy life.

These lessons will help teach that God hopes that his children are good. This is why he gave us the Ten Commandments, like a guide to attain this goal.

The Ten Commandments clearly specify the rules of conduct that the chosen people of God should follow to live in harmony, peace and prosperity.

Jesus said that He did not come to abolish the law, but to fulfill it. (Matthew 5:17) Also he told us to obey God because we love him not because we have to.

When your students learn to love God with all their heart, and their neighbor as themselves, they are also following the Ten Commandments.

Lesson 1
First Things First

Biblical References: Exodus 19:1-20:21; Matthew 5:17; Mark 12:28-34

Lesson Objective: That the students learn to express their love for God by giving their whole life to Him.

Memory verse: *"Love the Lord your God with all your heart and with all your soul and with all your mind and with all your strength. The second is this: 'Love your neighbor as yourself.'"* (Mark 12:30-31a)

PREPARE YOURSELF TO TEACH!

We as Christian education teachers have a huge responsibility, and also, a great privilege. Our responsibility is to plant evangelical seeds in the hearts of our students and help them on their walk with Christ. Our great privilege is to be the Lord's instruments and evangelize all of creation.

In this book you'll find teachings and activities that will help facilitate your work of evangelize. But remember, for these teachings to be effective it is so important to follow the direction of the Holy Spirit.

There are many things out there these days that compete for pre-teen's attention: friends, sports, music, fun activities, etc. All of these options can confuse kids' priorities since they don't know how prioritize in the first place.

With this lesson, they will learn that God should take first priority in any Christian's life.

God gave rules to his people to serve as a guide, and in this way they could live in holiness and harmony. As your students learn this commandment, they will understand that when they love God above all other things, everything else will come to fruition.

BIBLICAL COMMENTARY

Exodus 19:1-20:21. God gave the Ten Commandments to his people and clearly explained that he hoped he would be the most important thing in their lives. After rescuing them from Egypt, he helped them cross the Red Sea and took them to Mount Sinai to hear His words. Before giving them the Ten Commandments, God reminded them of everything that He had done for them and he asked for their love in return.

Their obedience of the Ten Commandments would be how they would show love to God in response to the pact that God had made with them. He hoped that they would be a holy people and the commandments would help them live holy. The rules didn't make the Israelites God's people; rather, they received the commandments because they were God's people.

Matthew 5:17; Mark 12:28-34. One time, a teacher of the law came to Jesus and asked him a question. When God gave the Ten Commandments to His people, the leaders saw to it that more rules were added to form a complete law. In the New Testament times, the Jews had 613 laws and commandments that they had to follow. Of those, 365 were negative, and 248 positive.

The answer that Jesus gave him ended in the central point of the Jewish system of laws: "love the Lord" (one single phrase taken directly from the Shema) "and love your neighbor as yourself". These are the basis of all the other commandments.

Jesus identifies love as the most important characteristic that someone could give to please God.

God loves us and gave us everything necessary to reconcile ourselves with Him. But it's necessary that we love him with all our heart, soul, mind and strength.

As Christians, we are not to worship idols because we know that that does not please God. But, are we giving God the place He deserves in our life?

God simply asked the Israelites to remember His laws and hoped they would respond with the same love and obey His commandments.

In the same way, our obedience to God should come from the love we have for Him.

Development of the Lesson

Welcome the students and let each of them introduce themselves, their age and what grade they are in (going into)

A lot of them probably already know each other and that's okay too. Regardless, it will help everyone get to know any new students and help the new students get to know their peers.

If you have a lot of new students, we suggest that you make up buzz words that will help you remember everyone's names easily.

Being that it is the first class of the year, it's probable that your students are still excited about everything they just did during their Christmas vacation and end of the year. Let them each give a short account of their time away from school. This will help them be able to focus on today's Biblical theme.

Classroom Rules

Explain to the kids that in an organized society, there are a series of rules that you should follow to maintain harmonious relationships. Then ask them what kind of rules they have. Listen to their responses.

Then, tell them that between all of you, you'll come up with Classroom Rules that all of you will follow during the year. We suggest that you let the students collaborate and assist by contributing their own ideas for rules. That way they won't feel like the rules are an imposition but will see them as things they helped make and will be more likely to follow.

Write on a poster the rules that you all decide on and hang it somewhere where everyone can see it for the rest of the year. We suggest that instead of saying things like "Don't run in class", say "Avoid running in class". In this way the children will receive the message without feeling reprimanded.

What do you think about the rules

Say to the students, "It's been a few moments since we decided on our class rules. In this activity we will dig a little deeper into rules."

Hand out the student worksheets and have them circle the answers that describe what they feel when they have to obey rules.

Concentration game

For this activity you'll need 30 white cards, separated into 15 pairs. On each pair of cards, draw a geometric figure (square, triangle, rectangle, etc.) or write a word (house, tree, flower, etc.)

To start the game, divide the class into two teams. Explain to them that the game will require concentration, while they put the cards on their table, face down. Ask a player from the first team to choose two cards and turn them over. If the figures/words are the same, they will keep the cards; if they are different, they turn the cards back over and it's the next team's turn.

Then, ask each member from the first team if they'd like to change the rules and how they would like to do so. Follow the new rules the next time you play. Then ask the second team how they would change the game and follow their rules.

Continue changing the rules each time you switch teams.

After the games finishes, ask them how they felt when the rules kept changing. Maybe they felt it was unjust, frustrating, or just that it was difficult to remember all of the rules.

Explain to them that in today's lesson they'll see why it's so important to obey the rules.

BIBLE STORY

It's important for everyone to bring their Bible to class. Tell the class that each week you'll be using it in class and that it'll be important to bring them home as well.

If some of the students don't have a Bible, they can share with their neighbor; figure out who you can talk to to see if you can supply the kids with Bibles. Another option would be to find people in your congregation who can donate Bibles to the students in your class.

After making sure that all the kids have a Bible that they can use in class, ask them to find Mark 12:28-34, and have a volunteer read it.

Then, divide the class into two teams, and have each group name a leader and a secretary. The activity that they'll be doing can be found on the second page of their activity sheet.

The first team should analyze and respond to the questions in group A, and the second group will do the same in group B. The secretary of each group will write down the answers on a piece of paper.

Then, each leader will choose a member of the opposite team to answer one of the questions that they answered. They can use the secretary's notes for help.

ACTIVITIES

What's more important?

For this activity you'll need magazines or used newspapers, scissors, glue and cardboard. Before bringing magazines to your class, make sure there are no inappropriate ads or articles.

Ask your students to find and cut out objects or people that are more important than God to many people. Then, give them time to glue them to their pieces of cardboard that they'll use for the next activity.

What idols do people worship today?

Ask the class to take a look at the things and people they cut out and answer the question on the next page of the student workbook.

Tell them: When people put things on pedestals in their life, they are not honoring God. Everything they love more than God is an idol.

Ask the students to give examples of idols that society adores (singers, famous athletes, TV personalities, style, money, etc.)

Read together Exodus 20:3-4 and talk about the significance.

Special cards

Ask your students to talk about specific ways that they can express their love for God and make Him first in their life. (Pray and read the Bible every day, be loving to their siblings, forgive those who've offended them, etc.)

Ask them to turn to the last page of their worksheet to write a card to God and tell Him how they'll honor and obey Him.

TO FINISH

Thank your students for attending class and remind them that in order to grow in their knowledge of God, it's necessary that they attend bible study regularly.

Ask them to pick up the materials that they used and that they help put things away in the room.

Conclude the class with prayer and challenge them to make God the top priority in their lives.

Power of Words

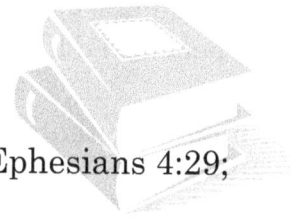

Biblical References: Exodus 20:7; Matthew 5:33-37; 12:35-37; Ephesians 4:29; Colossians 3:8-9

Lesson Objective: That the children evaluate how they speak and make sure their words honor God and their neighbors.

Memory verse: *"Love the Lord your God with all your heart and with all your soul and with all your mind and with all your strength. The second is this: 'Love your neighbor as yourself.'"* (Mark 12:30-31)

PREPARE YOURSELF TO TEACH!

How many times do we hear God's name used just like any other expression? It's very common for people to use the name of the Lord in vain and not even know what they're saying. Because of this, many children have grown up hearing phrases that use the Lord's name in vain. They probably think this is completely normal, and that's because they don't understand the significance of His name and the respect it deserves.

This lesson will help the students to understand why they should respect the name of the Lord and not use it in vain. His name is sacred and deserves all honor. The Ten Commandments prohibit the use of His name in vain. Unlike western culture, where words aren't as important, the Israelites thought that their words took life after they said them.

Help the students understand that the way they speak and express themselves reflects what is in their heart.

BIBLICAL COMMENTARY

Exodus 20:7. This commandment tells us clearly how God wants His children to express themselves. He warned the people of the importance of not underestimating the name of the Lord. "In vain" means that it has no value, or it's something without any importance.

In general, this commandment prohibits using the name of the Lord in an indiscriminate way. To use it in such an invaluable, false or deceitful way attributes those characteristics to God.

The Israelites considered the name of God so holy that they never mentioned it. But they used other names to reference Him, like Adonai or Jehovah. The high priest mentioned God's name only one time per year when he blessed the people on the day of atonement (Leviticus 23:27).

Matthew 5:33-37; 12:35-37. In New Testament times, the people used the name of God to make oaths valid. For this reason, Jesus prohibited that use as well. He wanted them to remember that the name of God is sacred and holy, and that all of us would be judged for the words we used.

Ephesians 4:29; Colossians 3:8-9. Paul expanded on this idea in his letters to the Christians that they should respect their brothers with their words.

Paul urges us to remove dishonest words from our vocabulary, including things like curse words, being sarcastic, complaining, insulting and making comments that hurt another's self-image.

But it's not enough to refrain from saying mean things. Proverbs 15:23 says: "how good is a timely word!" The Bible urges us to minster to others through the way we speak. When our words build others up, we are honoring God.

LESSON DEVELOPMENT

The wordless game

Write down short phrases on small pieces of paper and put them in a box or envelope. Explain to your students that each of them will take turns taking out a paper and try to communicate the phrase to others but without using any words.

Write sentences like: 'I need new shoes', 'I need a pencil', 'I'd like to eat', 'I'm thirsty', 'I'm tired', etc.

Emphasize that many times we can't recognized the blessings we have just from the spoken word because oftentimes, we make poor use of them.

What kind of words do you use?

Write on the board the following list of words, in pairs and underneath each other:

Good – bad; pretty – ugly; respectful – disrespectful; good – bad; agreeable – disagreeable; cheerful – angry; happy – sad.

Then, hand out paper so that they students can write down simple sentences with these words. Ask some students to read their sentences. Together, analyze how people respond to our words. For example: 'you look nice' and 'you look bad' are phrases that are alike; there's just one word that's different; determine how people react to hearing them.

Many times, we speak without thinking, and we hurt those who we're talking to. Today we will study how important it is to honor God with our words.

BIBLE STORY

Tell the student: Last Sunday we studied the first commandment that told us to prioritize God and honor Him above all things. In today's class we will study another important commandment.

Divide the class into three teams and assign each group the questions on the second student worksheet. Indicate to the students that they should read the suggested Bible passages to answer the questions.

When they are done, ask them to share their answers. If necessary, expand on the answers the students gave.

ACTIVITIES

Help the alien

The class should work on their activity sheet by helping the alien write a brief report about the ways that people on Earth should respect each other. It should be based on Matthew 5:33-37; 12:3537; Ephesians 4:29 and Colossians 3:8-9

Evaluate your words!

Give your students time to answer the self-evaluation card on their worksheet. Tell them that their answers are confidential, so they should work by themselves.

Challenge them to answer with honesty and figure out how they can do better in the areas where they have difficulty.

Solve the crossword puzzle

One more time, divide the class into small groups or pairs to solve the crossword puzzle on their activity sheets. This activity will serve to review some of the incorrect ways to use language that we use most often.

Check that they have the correct answers:

Horizontal

1. Words that are said with the intention of hurting someone (insults)

2. Intense emotion caused by something negative (anger)

3. Negative commentary about another person (criticism)

4. Indecent and obscene (vulgar)

5. Expression of discontent (complaint)

Vertical

6. Act of lying to hurt someone's reputation (slander)

7. Rumor about someone (gossip)

8. Cruel joking to offend or hurt someone (sarcasm)

9. Disdain or lack of appreciation for someone or something (contempt)

10. Indignation and uncontrollable anger (rage)

TO FINISH

Tell them to read "A Prayer about the words I use" on their student worksheet. Conclude by giving thanks to God for the gift of language, and ask Him to help you honor Him with the use of your words.

Stress the importance of attending the next class, and if there were new students in attendance, make sure to visit them or call them this week.

Lesson 3

A special day

Biblical References: Genesis 2:1-3; Exodus 20:8-11; Matthew 12:1-13

Lesson Objective: That all of the students understand that God wants us to use our day of rest to praise Him.

Memory verse: *"Love the Lord your God with all your heart and with all your soul and with all your mind and with all your strength. The second is this: 'Love your neighbor as yourself.'"* (Mark 12:30-31)

PREPARE YOURSELF TO TEACH!

Today's world is far busier and hurried than ever before. Have you ever thought that the days seem to be getting shorter? Our jobs seem to fill our calendars and our minds. And this isn't just the case with adults; teens and kids too are suffering negative consequences from being so active. School, sport practices, chores, homework and extra classes are only some of the multitude of activities that our pre-teens are doing for the majority of the week.

Of course, it's good to intellectually and physically stimulate our youngsters. But there is always the danger of saturating their lives with activities and not leave time for the most important thing: their relationship with God.

The students need to learn that God established the Sabbath so we could rest and concentrate our attention on Him.

Explain to your students that God gives us six days to work and complete our tasks. But it's our responsibility as God's children to keep the Sabbath holy and praise the Lord on the seventh day.

BIBLICAL COMMENTARY

Genesis 2:1-3. God is so wise. Even before man started to work, He had already put a day aside for resting and strengthening our walk with Him. Our Creator knows that we need a day of rest to renew our energy and strength. But this doesn't refer only to our physical strength. We also need to renew our spiritual strength.

Matthew 12:1-13. With frequency, the Pharisees accosted Jesus with questions referring to the Sabbath. These men of the law had converted this day, designed for the Lord, into a series of elaborate rituals that needed to be completed to the 't'. When Jesus healed a man who had a shriveled hand on the Sabbath, the pharisees criticized him, accusing him of breaking the law of God. They had given priority to their rituals and the law before the needs of humans.

Regardless, Jesus had the correct answer: "The Sabbath was made for man, not man for the Sabbath" (Mark 2:27).

God established the Sabbath so his children would relax from their daily to-dos. But the most important thing we can do is to dedicated time to praise Him and strengthen our relationship with Him.

LESSON DEVELOPMENT

Three questions

Write on separate pieces of paper each of the following questions. On the backside of the paper, write the number of the question, then hide them in different parts of the classroom.

- Question 1: What happens when people are too busy?
- Question 2: Why do you think people are so busy?
- Question 3: Is Sunday different than all the other days? Why?

Let the students find all the questions.

When they are found, they should answer them together. Listen to their answers and tell them that today in class they'll learn why Sunday is special.

BIBLE STORY

Read the passages ahead of time and tell the story in your own words.

Explain to your students the details that can confuse them (for example: who were the Pharisees and why was it so important for the Jews to keep the Sabbath). Let the students ask questions if they have any.

You can also ask the class for a couple of volunteers to read the study passages aloud and then talk about them with the whole class.

ACTIVITIES

The Capernaum News

Divide the class into small groups and tell them to pretend they are reporters or newscasters on Capernaum News. Like reporters, they should interview a main character of the Bible story from today and write up a short report about it.

The characters that should be interviewed are: the pharisees, the disciples, the man with the deformed hand, or Jesus.

Make sure that each group interviews a different character and they use their Bible to help write their report. Then have them read the conclusions on page 13 of their student worksheet.

The day of the Lord

Ask the students to read and converse about the situations mentioned on page 15 of their worksheets.

Ask them: Do you think that these kids are keeping the Sabbath holy?

Listen to their answers before moving on to the next activity.

How do you use the day of the Lord?

Guide the students to page 14 of the student worksheet. Ask them to write a list of activities that they do on Sundays, indicating how much time they dedicate and the type of activity (Family, school, recreational, etc.).

Then, let them put the letters in order to reveal other activities that glorify God on the day of the Lord. (Do good things, Worship God, Rest)

Use these activities to guide your students into reflecting on how they spend their time on Sundays.

Memorization ACTIVITIES

Instruct your students about the ways to perform the suggest manual labors suggested on page 16 of their books, following these instructions: cut the strip of paper with the Bible verses (p. 15) and cut out the white window in the top right corner. Then, fold the page following the dotted line and glue on the edges. Have them insert the text so that you can read the words through the window. Lastly, have them repeat the verse, phrase by phrase, while they slide the slip upwards to test that they are saying it correctly.

TO FINISH

Organize everyone into teams to clean the room, put away materials, etc. Finish with prayer and challenge them all to honor God by keeping the day of the Lord holy.

notes

Lesson 4

We need our parents

Biblical References: Exodus 20:12; Ephesians 6:1-3

Lesson Objective: That the students learn the significance of honoring their parents

Memory verse: *"Love the Lord your God with all your heart and with all your soul and with all your mind and with all your strength. The second is this: 'Love your neighbor as yourself.'"* (Mark 12:30-31)

PREPARE YOURSELF TO TEACH!

Nowadays, respect has ceased to be a form of constant behavior and has begun to be an obsolete word. It's common to see people not respect their authorities, institutions, elderly people, and even their own parents. What is so sad is that many students imitate this same behavior and their idea of respect is very skewed. As children grow up and become more independent, they often rebel against their parents. This rebellion is partially because of outside influences, their friends, styles and what they see on TV, etc.

It's common that in this phase, their parents are having difficulties communicating with their kids. Many children obey their parents because they have to, not because they love them. The two main commandments (Matthew 12:30-31) will be a great help in helping to better relationships between parents and their kids. After this lesson, students should understand that we honor God because we love Him, and we should also honor and respect our parents for the same reason.

It's sad that some young people come from homes where obeying their parents is not obeying God. In these cases, obeying God should be the priority. Be sensible about these situations and give thought-out advice.

BIBLICAL COMMENTARY

Exodus 20:12. The first four commandments are about our relationship with God. The next six are in regards to our relations with everyone else. Our relationship with people should follow the example set by our relationship with God.

Maybe a lot of people ask why God even made the fifth commandment. Why is honoring our parents the opener to the second part of the 10 Commandments? We can be sure that this commandment is placed exactly where it should be, since family is the basis of all of our interpersonal relationships. If the students have difficulty living with their family, they won't be able to interact correctly with other people.

Ephesians 6:1-3. In this passage, Paul reminds us that God delegated his authority to our parents to guide and correct their children. They can honor and obey their parents easily when they have the love of Jesus in their hearts. On the other hand, if parents show their children the love of God, they will respond back with love and obedience.

Why should we honor and obey our parents? First, Christian parents represent God. Your students should be making sure that they are honoring God by honoring their parents. Could you dishonor your parents who you can see and honor God who you can't see?

Second, our families are the center of society. When a family disintegrates, it affects the whole community.

Third, honoring our parents is a commandment with a promise, "that it may go well with you and that you may enjoy long life on earth." Frequent disobedience ends in bitterness and an early death. Rebellion against parents is also rebelling against God.

LESSON DEVELOPMENT

What does it mean to honor?

Write on the board the following definition: "To honor: respect someone; to praise or reward someone's merit; give honor to or celebrate" (RAE, Dictionary of the Real Spanish Academy)

Let some of the students express what it means to them to honor someone. Use a Bible with a concordance to find verses that talk about honoring.

Explain to them that we honor someone who deserves respect for what they have done or for what they represent. In today's class we'll learn why we should honor our parents.

My parents

Provide paper and color pencils for your students to draw or write a paragraph about what their parents represent to them.

Give them a few minutes to finish the activity and let a few volunteers share what they did. Tack up their pages to a piece of cardboard to put up on the wall.

Afterwards, tell them that having a good relationship with their parents isn't always easy. Regardless, God left us some precise instructions in the Bible to show us how we should treat them.

Be sensitive towards your students who have lost a parent or find themselves in a disintegrating family situation. Make sure they know that even though their parents aren't with them or aren't around, they still have people around that are in charge of taking care of them and educating them as if they were their own parents. If necessary, stay behind to talk with them after class.

To honor... what, who and why?

While you distribute the worksheets, ask your students, "Do you know anyone who has recently received a special recognition or an honorable mention?" Let them answer.

Then ask, "If you were to receive a prize or recognition and you were able to choose it, what would you want to receive?"

Then, have them turn to page 17 and on the three cards write the names of people they believe deserve recognition and why.

Allow the necessary time for them to complete the activity. Make sure that no one notes any famous people on their cards. We want to make sure that they are people from church, the community or even within their own family. Then have the students talk about who they chose and why. Pay attention to see if anyone includes their parents in their list.

Then say, "Many people should receive recognition for something they've done. There is a group of special people who God has commanded that we respect. We are going to read in the Bible about who these people are."

BIBLE STORY

Start the Bible story by saying, "Everyone has different opinions about how children should treat their parents. Many authors have written books about this theme. Today we are going to learn about the teachings in the New and Old Testaments about respect. We'll start with the Old Testament."

Ask your students to find Exodus 20:12 and have a volunteer read it.

Ask them, "What does God tell us in this passage about how children should treat their parents?" Listen to their answers.

Then, divide the class into pairs to continue with this activity. Have them turn to page 18 and look up the Bible passages and write the answers in the blank spaces.

Explain to them that in these scripture passages, God gives us rules on how we should treat our parents.

As a review, we suggest you divide your class into four groups and assign each group to each of the following passages: Matthew 15:3-6; Luke 2:51-52; John 19:25-27 and Ephesians 6:1-3.

Each group should improvise a brief presentation about how to honor their parents according to their passage.

ACTIVITIES

Everyone has something to say!

While the students go back to their seats, say, "Sometimes parents and kids don't agree. This is just a difference in opinion. In spite of that, children should try to understand where their parents are coming from and still be able to tell them what they are thinking. Have you ever had doubts about talking to your parents about something?" Listen to their answers and tell them, like every other human relationship, communication between parents and their children is fundamental in having understanding.

Ask them to write a message to their parents on page 19. Afterwards, tell them to write another one for friends who are going through the same situation and need help. For example, they can suggest ways to better their communication in their home, or different ways to honor their parents.

If they wish, you can allow time for them to share their messages with the group.

How can I respect my parents?

Turn to page 20. There they'll find a list of actions that show respect towards their parents. While they read each sentence, ask them to evaluate the frequency with which they complete those actions by putting an X in the column that corresponds with their answer.

A special coupon

Direct everyone's attention to the small part on page 20, to fill in the blank spaces on the coupon, writing how they can respect their parents during the week. (For example: do what my parents ask, clean my room without my parents asking, complete all my chores at home, etc.)

Provide scissors so they can cut the coupon out and take it home to give to their parents as a special gift.

TO FINISH

Review the Memory verse a few times. Then lead them in a time of prayer asking God to help them respect and obey their parents.

Sing some songs before leaving and challenge everyone to return next week.

notes

Lesson 5
What do you see?

Biblical References: Exodus 20:13; Matthew 5:21-22; Ephesians 4:26; James 1:19-20

Lesson Objective: That the students learn to submit their thoughts to God and not to let violence guide them.

Memory verse: *"Love the Lord your God with all your heart and with all your soul and with all your mind and with all your strength. The second is this: 'Love your neighbor as yourself.'"* (Mark 12:30-31)

PREPARE YOURSELF TO TEACH!

We live in a culture of violence. It just takes a quick look around to see how many ways of communication we are bombarded with on a daily basis, including magazines, books, video games, tv, theater, etc., making the viewing of violence something normal. By the time the majority of kids reach the age of 18, they've already seen thousands of deaths on TV.

Because of this, it's easy to become accustomed to this life of violence. It's important that throughout this lesson your students learn to not let themselves be influenced by the enemy. Every day they are confronted with violence in school, their neighborhood and maybe even in their home. Students are bringing more and more firearms into schools. Gangs are growing because students are joining them more and more. One in every five families are subject to domestic violence.

One of the Ten Commandments, "Don't kill," teaches us to value others. Jesus extended this rule to show His followers the relationship between hatred and homicide. The students need to learn to control their anger before it becomes violence.

BIBLICAL COMMENTARY

Exodus 20:13. Life is a gift that God gives us; because of that, taking it away from someone is like taking God's place. The Lord gave his people a specific commandment to not murder.

Ephesians 4:26. In this passage, Paul tells us that it's better to resolve problems before the sun sets. It's not as easy at it sounds, but we should try to not go to bed angry; if we do, this allows anger to stick around in our heart and it could turn into bitterness and resentment.

James 1:19-20. This passage contains advice on how to avoid problems that stem from ire and anger. It tells us that we should be quick to listen, slow to speak and slow to get angry. Your students will learn that violence produces more violence.

Pray that God directs the lives of your students and helps them avoid a life of violence.

LESSON DEVELOPMENT

Welcome your students and ask for a volunteer to pray for the opening of class. Explain to them that the lesson today has a very important theme, and they should pay very close attention to the activities and reading.

My eyes

In the middle of the board write "MY EYES" and ask the students to tell you what eyes help us do. Note all of the answers on the board, attaching them to "MY EYES" with arrows.

Then say, "God gave us our eyes as an amazing gift. Because of them, we are able to see and learn a lot. But sometimes, we use them incorrectly and we see things that fill our mind with sin. In today's lesson we'll tackle this theme."

My favorite TV shows

Have the students turn in the worksheets to page 21 and give them time to write down their five favorite TV shows, movies or video games. Then, have a few students tell the class what they wrote.

Tell them, "If we look around us we can find violence in almost every place, including books, tv shows, movies and video games.

What is violence?" Have them define it.

Then ask them to classify each program in the scale of violence found on the bottom of the page.

Talk about the results of the evaluation. How many programs don't show violence? How many have a high violence content? Pay special attention to the programs that are at 2-3 points.

Ask them, "Why do you think that so many of our favorite books, tv shows, movies and video games are so violent?" Listen to their answers and have a respectful conversation.

To conclude this activity, tell them, "Violence and anger are very common in our time. Today we'll study what the Bible says about that."

BIBLE STORY

Ask the students to pretend that they're in a city called "Megatropolis", but since it's new, there are no rules. Each one should participate by adding a rule to the city.

Write all the rules on the board and explain to them that these rules are important so we can live in harmony and have respect for each other.

Since the beginning of creation, God knew that it was essential to control humans' feelings. Because of that, in His Word, he wrote rules to help His people keep their feelings and emotions under control.

Divide the class into three teams and assign the questions on page 22 to each group. Tell them to answer the questions, based on the suggested Biblical passage.

After each group has finished, let a volunteer from each team read the portion of Scripture that was assigned to them and give the answers that they found.

Explain to them that God wants us to stay far away from violence. That's why it's important to be careful what we watch on TV or learn from our friends, and submit to the Biblical principles that help us live better.

ACTIVITIES

Don't get angry!

For this activity you'll need sheets of paper and pencils. Distribute the materials to the students and ask them to fold their paper in half (or draw a line down the middle separating the sides) In the first part they should write specific situations that make them angry. (People not paying attention to them, no time to play, they don't give me what I want, etc.)

In the second part they should write some suggestions on how to resolve the situation and control their anger.

Allow a few students to give their responses. Challenge the students to look to God for guidance on what to do so that anger doesn't control their emotions and actions.

Say no to violence!

Have the students sit in a circle and ask them how they can avoid violence in their lives. Write suggestions down on the board to arm them with a code of conduct that they can refer to in their day to day lives. (Don't watch tv shows that promote violence, don't buy video games with death in it, stay away from violent situations, etc.)

Write on a big piece of paper the suggestions and hang it in the room where they can all see it. Remind them that God wants to obey His commandments to live happily and in peace.

Memorization game

Write the parts of the Bible verse they are supposed to be memorizing (Mark 12:30-31) on different cards and hide them around the room before class starts. (When all the cards are found, the whole verse should be there.)

Ask the students to find the cards and put them in order as fast as they can. If you want to, you can divide the class up into teams.

Then, have them repeat the verse together a few times before you end the class.

TO FINISH

Pray by given thanks to God for his teachings today, and ask that He helps protect our eyes from everything that promotes violence and anger.

Challenge the students to live according to the 10 Commandments. If possible, call them or visit them during the week to encourage them.

Tell them that the next lesson is called "I'm Special" and it's about something very important. Dismiss the class with a praise song.

Lesson 6

I Am Special

Biblical References: Genesis 1:27-31; Exodus 20:14; Psalms 119:9; Matthew 5:27-28; Ephesians 5:3-4

Lesson Objective: That the students understand that God wants them to stay pure in His eyes.

Memory verse: *"Love the Lord your God with all your heart and with all your soul and with all your mind and with all your strength. The second is this: 'Love your neighbor as yourself.'"* (Mark 12:30-31)

PREPARE YOURSELF TO TEACH!

Your students are at a changing age. Every day they experience something new in every part of their life, including their body and emotions developing. In this stage, they are discovering that the opposite sex isn't as 'icky' as they originally thought, and they actually want to start relationships with them. It's a normal part of the growing process. That is why it's important that they learn what God's point of view is regarding sexuality.

Through all means of communication, your students will be continually bombarded with inadequate information about relationships, sexual or otherwise. Many of these communications treat these subjects in a way that is impure and improper. The enemy has charged himself with giving this inappropriate information to preteens and youngsters to assist them in making bad decisions in the realm of sex.

God wants us to live a holy life. Therefore, your students should learn that the sexual immorality that is promoted via ads, etc. is not acceptable before God. They need the teachings from the Bible.

BIBLICAL COMMENTARY

Genesis 1:27-31. God created man and woman and blessed them with sexuality. Sexual intimacy is a gift from God to human beings and it's something we should enjoy within the confines of His ordinances. Sex becomes something dirty when you start using it in ways for which it wasn't created. Your students need to know that God wants us to stay pure in his eyes. He wants to keep us from sexual temptations but in order for him to do that, we need to seek his guidance and direction.

Ephesians 5:3-4. In his letter to Ephesus, the apostle Paul talks about the importance of living a pure life. There he presents a list of six sins that should be far away from the life of a Christian: fornication, impurity, greed, lying, foolishness, and cursing.

In His Word, God warns us about the dangers of living out the things of this world and forgetting His precepts.

It's our prayer that God uses you to plant a seed in your student's hearts so that they, too, will wish to maintain purity.

LESSON DEVELOPMENT

Clean water and dirty water

For this activity, you'll need two glass vases, two cups of purified, clean water and two cups of dirty water.

Before the students arrive, put the two vases on a table and have the cups of water close by. For the dirty water, we suggest you add two spoonfuls of dirt or dark food coloring.

When the students arrive, have them sit in front of the table and start the class with a prayer.

26

Then, empty the clean water into a vase and the dirty water into the other. Tell them, "I want to share some water with you. Choose which one you'd like to drink." Obviously, everyone will choose the clean water. Ask them why they chose that one and listen to their answers. Say that when the water is dirty, no one wants to touch it, much less drink it. However, when the water is pure with nothing contaminating it, we can drink it with confidence.

In today's class we'll talk about something that contaminates mankind. Also we'll see what the Bible says about living a pure life.

Put the vases away to use them again later.

What do they sell?

Ask the students, "Do you remember some of the commercials you've seen on TV?" Let them answer and then ask, "How can we remember these so easily?"

After listening to a few examples, ask your students to look at page 23 of their worksheets and make a list of 5 commercials that they like.

Then ask them, "Why is it so easy for us to remember these?" Listen to their responses and write them on the board. "Are the people in them attractive? Are they dressed modestly? How do you feel when you see these images?"

Have them look at the illustrations on the worksheet page and have them circle the ones that use sexual immorality to promote their product and a '?' by the ones that don't.

While they work, say, "Last week we studied the influence of violence in our lives and how the things we watch and play make it seem like something normal. What we see and hear can give us the wrong idea about sexuality as well. Many commercials use images and messages that promote impure sexual conduct. But, the Bible teaches us something very different."

BIBLE STORY

Your students will learn the biblical truth much easier by getting into groups or teams and investigating, rather than just listening. So, we suggest you divide the class up into three groups and have each group answer a group of questions on page 24. Provide them with Bibles, dictionaries and any other resources you may have nearby.

Help them clear up any doubts that come up while working together and ask that they write down their answers.

When everyone is finished have all three groups share their answers with everyone else.

ACTIVITIES

Careful with the spiderweb!

For this activity you'll need a spool of thread, yarn or wool.

Arrange your students in a circle and place yourself in the center holding the skein of thread. Hand one end of the skein to one of the students and ask him to hold it firmly, while you circle around the group, entangling them in your 'spiderweb'.

While you do this, tell them that sexual temptation is much like a spiderweb. Although they probably only think it's an inappropriate thought or word, this sin, little by little, eventually envelopes them so that they are trapped. Explain to them that the web that the spider weaves is made out of a very sticky substance so that insects will stay stuck in there when they get close. That makes them easy prey for the spider.

The same thing happens with sexual temptations. So many people are attracted to them like a dangerous magnet. Regardless, the end is always a disaster.

Let the students try to get out by themselves, but if they can't, help them BEFORE you start the next activity.

What would you do?

This activity will help your students relate the theme to some situations that they'll encounter in their daily life.

Read out loud each situation and have the students respond with how they would handle it and move away from the temptation.

- While they prepared for a soccer match, Luis heard his teammates mocking a girl from their school. What would you do if you were Luis?

- Blanca invited Mariela to her house for a sleep over and to watch movies. The theme of the movies was only for adults (rated R). What would you do if you were Mariela?

- Diego invited Bruno to his house after school. After dinner, Diego took out some magazines. When Bruno saw the covers, he realized that they were pornographic magazines. What would you do if you were Bruno?

Memorization game

Use the same cards from the last class and put them on a table. Each participant should go to the table, take a card and stick it to the board, ensuring it's in the correct order from the Bible.

When they've finished, repeat the text a few times as a review.

TO FINISH

Show the students the vases of water from earlier and tell them that when sin contaminates someone, their heart looks like this dirty water. But when we decide to live like Christ and obey God's commandments, our heart is crystal clear, just like the purified water.

Guide them in a prayer asking God to help them stay away from these temptations and maintain their sexual purity.

Remember to invite them to the next class to study the lesson: If it's not yours, leave it alone.

notes

If it's not yours, leave it alone!

Biblical References: Exodus 20:15; Ephesians 4:28

Lesson Objective: That the students know that stealing is a sin and that it carries lots of consequences.

Memory verse: *"Love the Lord your God with all your heart and with all your soul and with all your mind and with all your strength. The second is this: 'Love your neighbor as yourself.'"* (Mark 12:30-31)

PREPARE YOURSELF TO TEACH!

Even though stealing is something pretty common in preteens and teenagers, some will say that they've never taken anything that wasn't theirs. Maybe they're telling the truth or maybe they have the wrong idea about what is stealing. Some don't know that stealing can be in the form of cheating in games, or copying someone else's work during tests.

Since personal image and being popular are so important to young people, they try to do whatever they can to gain acceptance from their peers.

Some are pressured to rob a store to show how brave they are. Others look for better strategies to goof off in class and become the center of attention.

It's important that the students understand that any sort of stealing is a sin to God, no matter if it's a magazine or a bank. Stealing will always bring negative consequences into their lives, and above all, their relationship with God will be broken.

BIBLICAL COMMENTARY

Exodus 20:15. The eight commandment is simple and direct: 'You shall not steal'. Sometimes we think we won't have a problem carrying this law out because we've never robbed someone. Regardless, some ignore that this commandment is much more than we could ever imagine. For example, the employee who takes things from the office, even if people don't see or notice, or the person who doesn't pay their taxes, the friend who borrows money without intending to return it and the student who cheats on an exam; all of these are forms of stealing.

The city of Israel had a concept of property much like ours. For them, property was an extension of the owner itself. So, if you stole property, it was a violation against the person themselves.

Robbing or stealing is a sin against people because we think only of our gain, we forget the needs of our brother or sister. But it's also a sin against God, because we are violating one of his commandments.

Of course, robbing and stealing always come with consequences, whether it's morally, emotionally, familial, even including legal. But the gravest of consequences is that this sin takes us farther and farther away from God.

LESSON DEVELOPMENT

Surprise!

Ask the students to put their valuables on a table in the front of the class (watch, ring, wallet, keys, etc.), and then return to their seats.

Show them all the objects and have some students comment on them. Then separate two objects from the group. Return the large group of valuables and keep the two that you took out.

Show the class the two items you kept. Let them know that you want to keep them because they are so pretty, then put them in your bag or pocket. The owners will not agree with what you just did, so take advantage of this time and ask them why.

Use this activity to help the students understand how people feel when they are robbed. Tell them, "It makes all of us unhappy to have things taken from us, especially when they are stolen from us. We all know that stealing is bad. In today's class we'll see what the Scripture says about stealing."

Raise your hands!

Ask your students to find page 25 in their worksheets and write down 5 objects they own that they wouldn't miss if they were stolen. Let a few volunteers say their answers.

Then, have them write down 5 objects that they don't want taken.

Ask them, "How would you feel if someone robbed you of an object that you have taken care of for a long time?"

Listen to their answers and explain to them that it doesn't matter the value of the object, stealing always makes people feel insecure. Today's lesson shows us what the Bible says about stealing.

BIBLE STORY

We suggest you use the activity on page 26 of the student worksheet to show this lesson's Biblical Truth.

Provide a Biblical dictionary so they can look up definitions for 'to steal' and 'restitution' and compare them with what is shown in their worksheet.

Then, gather them into small groups to answer the four questions, consulting the Bible passages. Give time at the end for them to share their answers with the rest of the class.

ACTIVITIES

Different types of stealing

Tell your students: "Often, we think that stealing means to take something that isn't ours, but stealing covers other actions that don't praise God. This activity with help us recognize some of them."

Have the students read the different kinds of stealing on their worksheet.

Steal: to take something that is not yours without paying for it.

Copy: to use another person's ideas as if they were your own.

Defraud or Swindle: to take something from someone by being tricky or deceitful .

Defame: to discredit someone, verbally or in writing, to damage their reputation.

Vandalism: to damage someone else's property on purpose.

Filch: to steal, especially something of small value.

Help them to understand that in order to obey the eighth commandment, our actions shouldn't fall into these categories. In this way we honor God and obey His Word.

Is it a sin?

Let the students read the situations described on pages 26 and 27 of their work books. Then discuss if the situations are breaking one of God's commandments.

If they want, they can work in pairs. Use the examples to illustrate the different ways that you can fall into sin.

Consequences of stealing

Give time for your students to read the sentences on their worksheets page 28. Ask them to think about each and write down possible consequences that each type of stealing could bring.

Without a doubt, you'll have a variety of answers. But, help them understand that any type of stealing is a sin and can affect our relationship with God. This is the biggest consequence.

Then reflect on the question: "How can you avoid these consequences?" Tell them that it's necessary to ask for forgiveness from God and the person that we hurt. The Bible shows us that restitution is very important. Leviticus 6:5 says, "They must make restitution in full, add a fifth of the value to it and give it all to the owner on the day they present their guilt offering."

Regardless, the most important way to avoid the consequences is walking away from this kind of this sin.

TO FINISH

To finish the class, have everyone make a circle so everyone can ask for prayer if they'd like. Have a couple of students pray on others' behalf.

Then give thanks to God for having given us codes of conduct that help us live correctly in His eyes.

Challenge them give up EVERY kind of robbing to maintain a firm foundation in their relationship with God.

Lastly, review with everyone the memory verse a few times and then sing a song or two of praise to end the class.

Lesson 8
Lying brings consequences

Biblical References: Exodus 20:16; Proverbs 12:22; Acts 5:1-10; Ephesians 4:25

Lesson Objective: That the students understand that lying has many consequences.

Memory verse: *"Love the Lord your God with all your heart and with all your soul and with all your mind and with all your strength. The second is this: 'Love your neighbor as yourself.'"* (Mark 12:30-31)

PREPARE YOURSELF TO TEACH!

Have you noticed that many people put a huge emphasis on honesty and the truth, but it only applies to others and not themselves? This attitude is common among young people. Even though they affirm that lying is wrong, they don't have a problem exaggerating a story or lying to please their friends. The hope of being accepted makes them distort the truth in order to fit in.

Our students need to learn to live a life of integrity because if they don't, they'll grow up without a single notion of honesty. In our declining society, our churches should enforce the teaching of biblical principles that help men and women become honest and holy.

BIBLICAL COMMENTARY

Exodus 20:16. When God gave this commandment to the Israelites, he knew the impact that it would have on the people. In a society that lived wandering through the desert, many of the crimes were punishable by death. Lying could bring someone to this end as well. The Hebrew justice was very strict when it came to moral issues and things relating to the integrity of a person.

Acts 5:1-10. The story about Ananias and Sapphira teaches us two very important things: When a person lies, it affects the relationship between the victim and the liar; it also affects one's relationship with God.

When Ananias and Sapphira tried to lie to the apostles, giving them less money than they had received for the land they had just sold, the were not just lying to God's servants, but also to the Holy Spirit. Their lie brought them the consequence of death, but above all, eternal separation from God.

LESSON DEVELOPMENT

What is lying?

Write on the board the following definition: "To lie is 'to say or manifest something in opposition of what you know; to feign; to falsify something; to break a promise; to break a pact'" (RAE).

Ask the students to read the definition and give some examples of what lying is.

Unbelievable but real

Pass out note cards or small pieces of paper to all your students and have them write down two acts that seem unbelievable but are real (they can be their own or someone in their family's). For example: "my uncle Fernando has a collection of 150 mechanical pencils" or "my little brother can move his eyes and his ears at the same time," etc. We suggest that you tell the students about this activity as soon as they get to class so they have some time to think about it.

Pick up the cards and read the contents out loud so they can try to figure out who wrote which one.

Ask them, "Why is it so hard to discern truth from lie?"

After listening to some answers, tell them that today they will be studying what the Bible says about lying.

BIBLE STORY

Have your students sit in a circle. Tell them "Today's Bible story shows us how lying enters the heart of a person and hurts their relationship with God."

Ask them to read Acts 5:1-10 in their Bibles or on page 29 of their worksheets.

Assign verses or paragraphs for each student to read. If you have a small group, one person can read a complete paragraph or the entire passage.

It's important that you clearly explain how Ananias and Sapphira's sin condemned them to death. Make a list of questions to start a conversation about the theme of lying and its consequences in the lives of preteens.

ACTIVITIES

Is it a lie?

Through this activity your students will learn that lying, much like stealing, presents itself in different ways.

Write the following words on colored cards: "holy lie," "gossip," "exaggeration," "perjury," "defamation." Hide the cards throughout the classroom so that everyone can find them.

When they've found all of them, stick them to the board and explain each of the words to them. It's important that the students know that lying isn't just saying something false but also the exaggeration of the truth, hiding the truth or distorting it, etc.

Would you believe these lies?

Divide the class into small groups and have them work on pages 30-31.

The first thing that they should do is write some situations that are examples of each kind of lie. Then have them write one or two consequences of what can happen in each scenario.

When all the groups are finished, have them talk about what they wrote. Then explain to them that lying always brings negative consequences that affect our relationship with people, and above all, our relationship with God.

Remember that it's always important to verify information that your students have written on their worksheets and spend more time on the concepts that they have doubts on.

The test of truth

Turn the page and ask the students to look at page 32. Tell them, "Read each of the sentences and decide if they are true or false. Write the number 1 by the sentence if it's true, and a number 2 if it's false."

Then, have them read the sentences again, but this time replace "many teens" with "me/I". Remind them that they should be honest in answering the questions. If they realize that they are more inclined to lie, tell them that God wants to help them be honest and always tell the truth.

What does God say about lying?

Ask your students to find and read Proverbs 12:22. Explain to them that even though this is from the Old Testament, God still shows us how much he detests the lips of liars, but he delights in people who tell the truth.

Then, have them find and read Ephesians 4:25. Tell them that Paul taught the Christians to speak the truth and be honest with others.

Use the concordance of the Bible to find other passages that are related to lying that can serve your students to help them understand this Biblical truth.

TO FINISH

Urge your class to always speak the truth in order to keep God's commands. Remind them again that lying has consequences, and worse then everything, it deteriorates our relationship with God.

Take some time to listen to all of the prayer requests, and don't forget to pray for all the students who missed class or are sick. Also, ask that the Lord helps them (and yourself) to always speak the truth and avoid lying and deceit.

Invite the students to the next class to study the last lesson of the unit.

Lesson 9

Don't Envy

Biblical References: Exodus 20:17; Matthew 6:19-21, 24-31; Philippians 4:10-13, 19; Hebrews 13:5

Lesson Objective: That the students understand that it is important to avoid envy.

Memory verse: *"Love the Lord your God with all your heart and with all your soul and with all your mind and with all your strength. The second is this: 'Love your neighbor as yourself.'"* (Mark 12:30-31)

PREPARE YOURSELF TO TEACH!

It only takes one look around our surroundings or through our phones to remind us that we live in a materialistic society. Our success isn't measured by our spirituality, intelligence or integrity, but by our material possessions and our economic position. Neighbors and peers compete with one another to see who can have the better house, the most expensive car, more clothes, more jewels, etc.

Wanting to have things isn't bad, but wanting others' things, envying their material prosperity or doing everything you can to gain material things is dangerous and turns into envy.

Preteens are aware of this. Even school can become a place where they want to bring and show off their most special belongings. In this lesson they'll learn that God's commandments tell us to not covet or envy the things that belong to others; envy is another sin that separates us from God.

BIBLICAL COMMENTARY

Exodus 20:17. God gave this commandment to the Israelites to help them live in harmony in their community. The commandment prohibits the desire to want things that others possess. It's important to know that many times, envy causes us to violating other commandments.

The Hebrew word for envy means "want" or "want for yourself." Wanting something you don't have isn't bad, but when it becomes an obsession, we fall into the trap that is envy.

If we envy something, we become unsatisfied with what we have, and we begin to look all over for something that will satisfy our "need."

In the New Testament, God reminds us to stay way from envy: "Keep your lives free from the love of money and be content with what you have" (Hebrews 13:5a).

But the most important thing to understand is that possessions don't make us happy, but joy comes from knowing that God promises to never leave or forsake us.

LESSON DEVELOPMENT

General Review

Today we are concluding the most extensive unit of the year, so we suggest that you have a review of the Commandments with your students. For example, you can organize a small round table to discuss why it's important to keep God's commandments. Or get 10 volunteers and have each of them say a Commandment out loud.

I want everything!

For this activity you'll need sheets of paper, glue, scissors and old magazines.

Put the materials on the table and give a piece of paper to each student. Ask them to look through the magazines for pictures of things they want to own, then cut them out and glue them to the paper. We suggest that you have enough magazines for everyone.

Don't be surprised if one sheet of paper isn't enough for all the things the students want that are really materialistic. Remember, we live in a society where a person's value depends on what they own.

Then ask them why they chose those items, why they need them, and what they'd use them for. More likely than not, they'll respond with a simple, "because I want them" and not have a logical reason.

Use this activity to help them understand that wanting something isn't bad. But when we begin to obsess about things and will do whatever we must to get them, that's when envy sets in and that's when we get into trouble. Tell them, "A lot of times we say we need something, but in reality we just want it. The Bible tells us what happens when we want things that others have: it's called envy or coveting. Today we'll study what envy is and why God prohibits it."

BIBLE STORY

Want what you have.

Direct your students' attention to page 34 in their books. Separate them into small groups so they can answer the six suggested questions, in a Biblical way.

Once the students are finished, talk about each answer and emphasize the teachings from the Old and New Testaments about envy.

If the space on page 34 isn't enough for them to answer the questions, make sure to provide them with more paper.

ACTIVITIES

Wants and needs

Write on the board the following list of objects, one underneath the other, in a column. Then ask some volunteers to come up front and write "W" next to the things they want and "N" next to things they need.

The words are: shoes, pet, bicycle, food, video games, pants, jewelry, the best watch, doll, etc.

You can add words to the list if you want, depending on how much time you have and how many volunteers you have.

Slaves to envy

Have the students open their books to page 33. Give them time to write in the spaces, next to the chain, the stages a person goes through from wanting something until he commits a crime to get it.

Some of the stages can be:1) See and want an object that someone else owns; 2) Decide to take the object; 3) Plan out how to take it; and 4) take it.

Make sure to emphasize that envying or coveting something is what breaks the commandment, like don't kill or don't lie.

Antidote for envy

Ask the students' parents to help the students bring in soda-like bottles that are clean and empty for class. You'll need one for each student.

Cut pieces of paper and give several out to each student along with a bottle. Tell them that on each piece of paper they should write something that they are thankful to God for. (Example: 'I give thanks to God for my

parents,' 'I give thanks to God for my house,' 'I am thankful for my toys,' 'I'm thankful for the flowers,' etc.)

And have them write on one of the slips of paper "Antidote for envy." Then ask that they glue it to the outside of the bottle. Then they can put all the things that they are thankful for inside the bottle.

Tell them that when they are discontent and feeling a strong want to possess something that doesn't belong to them, open the bottle and remove the slips of paper. Then they can read all of the blessings that they receive daily from God and they'll learn to be happy with what they have.

Avoid temptation

For this activity you'll need a deflated balloon for each student and a piece of yarn.

Hand out the balloons to each student and have them blow them up and write on them the temptation that they deal with most often that could lead them to breaking one of the Ten Commandments. (Example: lie to my peers, cheat in a game, take money from my mom, etc.)

Then tell them to take their piece of yarn and tie one end to the balloon and one end to their ankle.

Stress that our Christian friends help us avoid temptation. Tell them that when you give the signal, everyone should try to pop their friends' balloons. Remind them to be careful and not to hurt their friends' ankles.

When all the balloons have been popped, give them a moment to go around picking up all the trash and throw it away. Then tell them to sit and explain to them that with God's help and the support of their friends from church, they can defeat temptation and follow God's laws that he's given us through His Word.

TO FINISH

Open the Bible and have everyone read Exodus 20:1-17 together as a final review. Then pray, giving thanks to God for having given us these laws that help us live correctly and obey His will.

Distribute all of their activities and work they completed during these nine classes and have them bring them home. Challenge them to obey and respect God's commandments in their daily lives.

Tell them that in the next unit they'll learn about someone who suffered a lot but learned a mighty big lesson.

GOD IS WITH YOU

Biblical References: Job 1:1-22; 2:1-12; 4:1-8; 8:1-6; 11:13-17; 32:1-5; 33:8-14; 38:1-11; 40:1-9; 42:1-17; Joshua 7-8

Unit Text: *"I can do everything, through Christ who gives me strength."* (Philippians 4:13)

Unit Purposes:

This unit will help the students to:

- Recognize the sovereignty of God and trust Him in difficult times, even if they do not understand why they have to deal with problems in the first place.

- Appreciate God's presence in the midst of difficult times.

- Decide to follow God, and in this way avoid the consequences of their past poor decisions.

Unit Lessons:

Lesson 10 – Job's Suffering

Lesson 11 – Why did Job Suffer?

Lesson 12 – Where was God?

Lesson 13 – Obeying God is worth it

Why do youth need to learn this unit?

It's common that students have heroes and people they admire. In this Unit, they will study the lives, lifestyles, and the decisions made by two people in the Old Testament that are worthy of admiration.

In this world full of injustices and suffering, we are confronted daily with problems that affect how we feel and think. There are familial problems, economic problems, natural disasters, sickness, death, etc. Your students aren't exempt from walking "through the valley of death". Regardless, the Word of God is clear. Through Job's example we understand that even through the most adverse times, God rewards the just.

God has control over everything and, being the sovereign One, He doesn't need to explain His actions. When your students experience difficult times and suffering, they probably ask why it's happening to them. In these times, even though God may not respond to them in person, they can remember the story of Job, knowing that God has control over all situations. Besides that, they'll be learning that God can give them the power and the strength to overcome things and continue believing in Him.

Job's Suffering

Biblical References: Job 1:1-22; 2:1-10

Lesson Objective: That the students learn that God is in control of all situation, regardless of how difficult they seem.

Memory verse: *"I can do everything, through Christ who gives me strength."* (Philippians 4:13)

PREPARE YOURSELF TO TEACH!

We all know, whether you're an adult of kid, life isn't always fair. Many times, students will become very discouraged and wonder why they have to go through such problems. It's important that they understand that every person in the world goes through things that are hard, and confront complicated situations that need to be resolved. Some of these are results of our own decisions, and some occur simply because we live in a sinful world.

The students should understand that as Christians, we need to have a different attitude towards our problems. We serve a sovereign God who has control over the whole world; he still gives us the freedom of choice. Therefore, Christians still suffer consequences for their decisions. Whatever the reason for the problem, Christians should trust God and recognize that He has infinite power.

BIBLICAL COMMENTARY

Job 1:1-22; 2:1-10. The divine court was in session and Satan entered and told God that Job was a just man only because he had been blessed with so many material goods. He accused God of buying Job's loyalty, and told him that if he took everything from him, Job would curse God. The Lord, confident in Job's pure heart, accepted Satan's challenge and permitted him to test Job's loyalty. But God put a limit on the actions of Satan.

So all of a sudden, Job lost everything: his children, possessions, flocks, heath and his prestige. But through everything, he continued to trust in God; during his long tests, Job never turned away from Him.

The important part of this story is Job's reaction when faced with a terrible situation. Throughout these lessons, God wants to show us how to confide in him and bear through trials like this by leaning on Him

LESSON DEVELOPMENT

Wants and needs

Divide the board into two columns. Over one write the title "Wants" and "Needs" over the other. Let the students write a list of things they want and things they need. Talk about the difference in needing things and wanting them.

Problems!

For this activity we suggest that you provide play-dough or something moldable. Have the students make something that represents the kinds of problems they encounter. (Example: a heart if they face emotional problems, a tomb if they recently lost a family member, etc.)

Let each student that wants to explain what they made and what it means to the rest of the class.

Bad news bulletin

For this activity you'll need old newspapers, cardboard, glue, scissors and colored markers.

Before bringing in the newspapers, be sure to go through them and make sure that there is nothing in them that is offensive or violent, pictures or words.

In class, spread out all the materials on one table. Let the students work in small groups. Have one student from each group gather the needed materials and then they can start working on making a bulletin board of bad news.

They should look for articles about tragedies or problems, cut them out and glue them to the cardboard. Make sure they each put a title on their bulletin board. When everyone has finished, give the opportunity for each group to explain the content of their work.

Then have a conversation about some different reasons that people today experience so much suffering. Write the reasons on the board while they take turns talking.

Why do people suffer?

Ask a volunteer to help distribute the worksheets to the other students.

Then ask, "Why do bad things happen to Christians?"

Let them talk about the headlines that appear on page 35.

Tell them, "We can't figure out why all of these tragedies happen. In today's Bible story we will learn about a person who loved God. Regardless, terrible tragedies happened in his life.

BIBLE STORY

Ask let the students to take turns reading aloud the story of Job, whether it's from the Bible or from pages 36 and 37 of the student worksheet.

If you wish, they can write on the board a list of all the tragedies that happened to Job, from the loss of his earthly possessions to the terrible sickness that came upon him.

Be alert to what the students are doing/talking about in case any doubts or problems come up between classmates.

ACTIVITIES

How did Job react?

Direct the students' attention to pages 36 and 37 of their worksheets. Ask them to underline the verses that show Job's reactions to the bad news/bad things that happened to him.

Then ask, "How do you think you would've reacted if those things had happened to you? Would you have shown as much faith as Job?"

Remind them that the most important part of this story is that no matter what terrible things happened to Job, he never lost faith in God.

Who is in control?

Ask them to read the story one more time and this time, underline the sentences that show that God had control over what happened to Job.

Explain to them that when Christians go through difficult times, they shouldn't blame God. It is a reminder that we live in an imperfect world, full of sin and injustice. However, sometimes we suffer over our own bad decisions.

Be a bridge.

Turn the page and you'll find an illustration of a bridge that unites God and people. In the water space have the students write down some problems that they are facing.

Ask them what helps us confide in God, even when things go from bad to worse. The answer is "FAITH". Write the word on the bridge and talk about its meaning.

Challenge the students to remember that God is always in control of those situations, even as difficult as they look.

TO FINISH

Review Philippians 4:13, and challenge them to repeat it when they are feeling down-trodden or that their problems will overtake them. Guide them in prayer and intercede for their requests on their behalf.

We suggest that you start a "Prayer Wall" where they can write their prayer requests and the answers to their prayers.

At dismissal, make sure you invite them to the next class.

Why did Job suffer?

Biblical References: Job 2:11-12; 4:1-8; 8:1-6; 11:13-17; 32:1-5; 33:8-14.

Lesson objective: That the preteens learn that difficult situations are not always a punishment from God.

Memory Verse: *I can do all this through him who gives me strength* (Philippians 4:13).

PREPARE YOURSELF TO TEACH!

It is very likely that not all young people will face problems as serious as Job's. However, each person experiences adverse situations that are out of their control and disturb them.

Maybe some come from divided homes and feel guilty, or have suffered the death of a loved one, or are sick. Maybe some are or have been victims of abuse, and feel inferior.

Remember that preadolescents do not always easily express their feelings and thoughts, but on the inside they may have questions and feelings overwhelming them.

Take this lesson as an opportunity to remind them that problems are usually not a punishment from God.

On the contrary, most of the times they are the result of someone's bad decisions. Job was not guilty of what happened to him, but he decided to continue trusting in God and to wait for his help.

Remind them that what is important is not the gravity of the problem or where it comes from, but knowing that everything can be overcome through Christ, the one who strengthens them.

BIBLICAL COMMENTARY

Job 2:11-12; 4:1-8; 8:1-6; 11:13-17; 32:1-5; 33:8-14. Three of Job's friends went to see him after they heard what had happened to him. When they arrived, it was hard to recognize him. Their friend, once healthy and cheerful, had become a disfigured and depressed man.

His friends showed their sadness by tearing their clothes and putting ashes on their heads. Then they sat with him for seven days without saying a word.

When they finally spoke, each one gave Job a different "recipe" as the solution to his problem. They did not understand why a righteous man might be suffering such a punishment. But all their ideas were wrong.

Eliphaz, the oldest and most respected, spoke first and said that people reap what they sow.

Job expressed his disagreement at those words. He assured him that he had done nothing wrong.

Bildad became angry, and said that Job was irreverent. He told him that God was just and that Job's children had died as a result of his sin.

Zophar, also thinking that Job had sinned, told him to repent and restore his relationship with God.

Job was saddened by his friends' attitude. Instead of comforting him, they had caused him more problems.

However, his faith was not broken, and he continued to declare that he trusted in God, despite the problems and suffering.

LESSON DEVELOPMENT

Best Friends

Provide your students with colored pencils and paper so they can draw and describe their best friend.

Then, give everyone time to come forward, stick their drawing on the board and briefly review the characteristics of the person they chose, and mention why they are friends.

Tell them that friends are a support in times of trouble. However in today's lesson, we will talk about three friends who, instead of comforting and helping, caused more complications.

Where do you seek advice?

Hand out the student worksheets, and ask your class: Who do you turn to for advice? Listen to their answers.

Ask them to look at page 39 of their worksheets and answer the four questions, choosing one of the three options available.

Explain that sometimes we do not receive good advice because we do not ask the right people.

In today's Bible story, we will learn about three of Job's friends who went to him to give him advice. Pay attention to learn if the advice they give him was good or bad.

BIBLE STORY

Have your students sit in a circle, and review last week's story.

Then, use the following introduction for today's topic: Job was very sad, sitting on ashes and covered with sores. Three of his friends went to visit him and were so sad to see him in that condition. Then they sat with him for seven days, without uttering a single word.

Then, one by one, they began to speak.

Direct the group's attention to page 40 of the worksheet. Ask four volunteers to read the paragraphs that correspond to friends.

ACTIVITIES

Were they right?

Use the activity on page 41 to review the Bible story. Ask your students to discuss the seven suggested questions in groups of three or four and write the answers in the blanks.

Then, read Job 33:9 aloud, giving time for them to write a brief testimony about Job's life in their own words.

Calamity or consequences?

Have some dictionaries on hand for your students to look for the definition of the words "calamity" and "consequence". Write them on the board.

Then discuss which of the situations on page 42 are a calamity or a consequence of poor decisions (for example: lung cancer is a consequence for those who have the habit of smoking cigarettes or other products that contain tobacco).

Be careful to help the preadolescents answer each of the questions correctly.

A special guest

Look for a person in your congregation who has faced a difficult situation (for example: an illness, the death of a loved one or they have lost their job). Ask them to tell the class how God helped them through it. This activity will allow students to connect the biblical truth to real life.

TO FINISH

Explain to the group that sometimes unpleasant events occur to us as a result of sin and disobedience. However, sometimes we suffer without an apparent reason, as was Job's case.

Throughout Job's story, we learned how he faced the situation and continued trusting in God, despite what happened to him.

Form a circle of prayer and intercede for the group's requests. Then, review the memory verse, and dismiss the class by singing a song.

Lesson 12

Where was God?

Biblical References: Job 38:1-11; 40:1-9; 42:1-17

Lesson objective: Preteens learn to trust in the power of God in the midst of consequences.

Memory Verse: *I can do all this through him who gives me strength.* (Philippians 4:13).

PREPARE YOURSELF TO TEACH!

At some point in our lives we have all wondered why certain situations occur. We want to know the cause of tragedies that we cannot understand or control: the death of a young man, the serious illness of a mother with small children, or the natural disaster that devastates cities, leaving behind death and destruction. And we ask ourselves: "Why, Lord?"

The book of Job does not say why events like these happen, nor does it explain why human beings suffer. However, it teaches us to trust in the almighty God, creator of heaven and earth.

It is important that preteens have an adequate concept of God. They must learn that His power goes beyond our human understanding, and that, although situations are often disastrous, he is faithful and will not leave his children helpless.

BIBLICAL COMMENTARY

Job 38:1-11; 40:1-9; 42:1-17. Job felt that God had been unfair and abandoned him in the midst of his problems. However, despite his complaints, he continued to believe in the sovereignty of God.

The Lord reminded Job that he had control of nature and that he had always been by his side, even though he had not noticed.

Job, in understanding his insignificance in comparison with the majesty of God, repented of his complaints and accusations. He understood that the ways of God are beyond the reach of human understanding, and that only He knows the reason of all situations.

When the trial was over, God blessed Job, giving him more sons and daughters, restored all his possessions and multiplied his cattle. The Lord showed Job his faithfulness, giving him more wealth and prosperity than he had before.

The book of Job does not answer why people suffer. However, it gives a message of encouragement to those who go through difficult situations, showing that faith can thrive even in the midst of confusion and doubt. It also reveals that God works in the midst of the most terrible circumstances because his power has no limits.

Many years after Job, another man suffered without deserving it. It was Jesus who suffered and died on a cross, but his suffering was the price of our freedom and our forgiveness.

God honored Jesus. Through the example of Jesus, He teaches us to be faithful and obedient in the midst of suffering.

LESSON DEVELOPMENT

Symbols to remember

For this activity you will need paper and colored pencils. Distribute the materials for your students to make a symbol (logo-type) that represents Philippians 4:13. When the work is finished, hang them on the walls of the room as reminders of the memory verse. At the end of the class, everyone will be able to take their work home and place it in their room.

Decisions and consequences

Write the following phrases on cards:

- Watching television instead of doing homework.
- Stealing a candy, instead of buying it.
- Telling lies, instead of telling the truth.
- Bicycling in the opposite direction of traffic.
- Making fun of a disabled partner.

- Cheating on a school exam.
- Spreading a false rumor about someone.
- Hiding something you broke to avoid consequences.
- Keeping dirty clothes under the bed instead of cleaning your room.
- Playing with your friends instead of helping your mom like she asked.

Keep all the cards in a box. Ask a volunteer to come forward and take out a card. Then read the phrase out loud and give a brief explanation about what the consequences of that action would be.

When you have read all the cards, explain that many times, suffering is the result of bad decisions we make. However, as in Job's story, we will occasionally face suffering without any apparent reason except that it will help strengthen our faith and trust in God, as we will study in today's lesson.

Important Decisions

Have your students look at page 43 of the worksheet, and allow time for them to write a list of nine decisions they have made, and what helped them make those decisions.

Talk about the lists they made. Write the most common answers on the board regarding what/who helped them make that decision (for example: scripture, parents, friends, teachers, etc).

BIBLE STORY

Before starting the story, take a few minutes to review what you studied in the previous lessons.

If your class is large, divide it into three groups. Assign Job 38:1-11 to the first group, Job 40:1-9 to the second, and Job 42:1-6 to the third. Tell them that each group should read their passage and write the two most important points they find.

Allow them to work 8 to 10 minutes on this activity. Afterwards, each group will come forward and present their conclusions to the others. If you think they will not be able to finish in that time, do the activity with the whole class instead of dividing it into groups.

After listening to the conclusions, make sure that the concepts have been made clear or provide more information on the subject.

ACTIVITIES

What did Job think? What do I think?

Use the activity on pages 44 and 45 to enrich today's lesson. Divide students into two teams to answer the suggested questions.

The first team will analyze and answer the questions on page 44, while the second one will work with the questions on page 45.

Then, both teams will read their answers and write them on their worksheets. The important thing about these activities is for students to talk and reflect among themselves. This exercise will expand their learning and help them retain the truths of the lesson.

Emergency!

Show your students some items that are used for first aid or responding to an emergency (for example, band-aids or bandages, gauze, a flashlight and a fire extinguisher).

Explain that these objects are used in case of an emergency. For example, when there is a fire, the extinguisher helps put it out, so it is advisable to have it on hand.

The same happens in our Christian life. When we face suffering and we are in an emergency, there are a series of procedures we must follow: pray, read the Bible and wait with confidence for the Lord's response.

Just as the extinguisher is used to put out the fire, prayer helps us to ease the pain in times of suffering. Encourage preteens to seek God during difficult times, and to exercise their trust in him, even if the circumstances seem terrible.

What was the most important thing Job learned?

Ask students to read from their worksheets (page 46) making the necessary pauses. Let them then talk about the importance of each of these affirmations. Let them know that when they obey the Word of God, pray, love their neighbors and are faithful, God will help them come out victorious from the problems they face.

TO FINISH

Review the memory verse and give thanks to God for this lesson. Have a short time of worship before you say goodbye, and do not forget to invite students to the next class for the last lesson of this unit.

Obeying God is worth it

Biblical References: Joshua 7—8.

Lesson Objective: That the students learn that obeying God strengthens our relationship with him.

Memory Verse: *I can do all this through him who gives me strength.* (Philippians 4:13).

PREPARE YOURSELF TO TEACH!

We are all aware that we live in a liberal society. Many parents refuse or fear to discipline their children. Others are so busy that they prefer to ignore the misbehavior of their children instead of taking the time to correct them. As a result, many young people are inclined to disobedience.

It is normal for students to feel that it is unfair for someone to correct them while others are misbehaving.

Everyone needs to know that God demands obedience, and that deliberate disobedience is a sin and has consequences. Many times preteens do not understand that their actions can affect others and themselves. They must understand that disobedience is not an isolated behavior; on the contrary, it affects many areas of our life and even our family. Through this lesson, help them understand that obedience is the only sure way not to suffer the consequences of disobedience.

BIBLICAL COMMENTARY

Joshua 7—8. Joshua was a great leader for the Hebrew people. He had many of Jesus' characteristics: he lacked selfish ambitions, he was not guided by hatred and revenge, and his goal was to do God's will. Because of his character, God chose him as Moses' successor and leader of the Israelites.

Israel's victory over Jericho illustrates the results of obeying God. The Israelites did not have to prepare complex war strategies, nor put the best men at the head of the battle. They just followed God's instructions and trusted in his power. However, Achan's story also reminds us of the consequences of disobedience. Achan broke the covenant with God. He stole objects that were forbidden to the Israelites (they were objects that God had ordered them to destroy). This story shows us how sin can affect a community. Achan's confession and punishment illustrate how serious disobedience was for the people of God.

Disobedience brings serious consequences, while obedience brings peace, forgiveness and restoration to those who believe in God.

LESSON DEVELOPMENT

Who was Joshua?

After welcoming your students and praying with them to kick off class, divide them into pairs or trios to find all the possible information on Joshua. Their main resource will be the Bible, but if possible, provide dictionaries and Bible commentaries.

Each team will briefly report what they researched about this Bible character. Tell them that this last unit lesson will deal with this servant of God.

You're the judge!

Ask two volunteers to help you distribute the student worksheets, and then turn to page 47.

Choose three children to read the situations out loud. Then together discuss whether the verdict was fair or unfair, and why.

Then tell them: In every situation, there was someone who disobeyed and suffered the consequences of their actions. Sometimes, even if we have done nothing wrong, we suffer the consequences of disobedience of a person in the group. In today's story, we will see what one man's disobedience caused an entire nation.

Follow the instructions

Hand out paper and pencils for your students to draw. For this activity, they must obey the instructions that you will give them. Explain that they must follow the instructions so that all the drawings end up being the same.

Choose figures that are easy to make. For example: In the upper right corner draw a circle; then draw a horizontal line in the middle of the sheet; Now, join that with the circle by drawing a vertical line, etc.

Allow everyone to show their drawings and compare them. Explain that in order to reach a common goal, instructions must always be followed perfectly. In today's Bible story, we will study about one man who obeyed God and another who decided to do wrong and received a terrible punishment.

BIBLE STORY

Ask your students to sit in a circle, and tell them: In the previous three lessons, we studied Job's life and the terrible pain he faced, even though he was a righteous man. Today we will talk about a man who, like Job, trusted God in difficult times, and another character who decided to sin and suffered severe consequences.

With the Bible open to the passage, retell the story of Joshua in the defeat of Jericho and Achan's sin. Emphasize that Jewish laws were very strict regarding obedience and loyalty to God, and that is why Achan received that terrible punishment.

ACTIVITIES

Joshua, the leader

Depending on the number of students, divide them into pairs or small groups. Assign them a question on page 48 to answer, based on what they learned in the Bible story. Allow them to consult their Bible to corroborate the information.

Then, give time to report the answers with each other and complete the exercise.

Follow Joshua's example

On page 49, tell students to circle the adjectives that describe Joshua's personality. Then, compare them with the personality of Jesus.

Write on the board the adjectives that the majority chose. Emphasize that it is important to ask God to help you be honest, obedient, humble, responsible and courageous, like this Bible character.

Consider and answer!

Divide the board into three columns. In the first, write: What are the consequences of disobeying God? In the second: What are the benefits of obeying God? And in the third: Why does God want us to obey Him?

Ask some volunteers to come forward and write the correct answers. After having reviewed them all, give them time to write them in the corresponding space of their worksheets.

Medical Exam

On page 50, ask your students to fill in the spaces with the required information. Tell them not to look at their classmates answers, because it is an exercise of personal reflection. Therefore, they must answer honestly.

You can explain that just as you go to the doctor to examine you when you have physical problems, you also need to review your spiritual health and ask God to restore the weak areas that need to be strengthened.

TO FINISH

Guide them in a time of prayer, and intercede for the special requests they have. Ask the Lord to help students to be faithful in the midst of problems, and to always trust in the sovereignty and power of God.

Hand back the work they have done during this unit, and encourage them to attend the next class. Remind them that next week they will begin the unit entitled "A great event".

A GREAT EVENT

Biblical References: Matthew 21:1-17, 23-27; 26:14-16; 27:11-26, 32-66; 28:1-20; Mark 14:53-63; Luke 22:39-62; 23:4-12; John 18:12—19:16.

Unit Verse: *Jesus said to her, "I am the resurrection and the life. The one who believes in me will live, even though they die; and whoever lives by believing in me will never die* (John 11:25-26).

The Purpose of this Unit

This unit will teach preteens to:

- Understand that Jesus endured an unjust judgment and death on the cross out of love for us.
- Recognize that Jesus' sacrifice was enough to forgive our sins and cleanse us from all unrighteousness.
- Know that Jesus, the Son of God, came to earth to save us.
- Make the decision to accept Christ as their personal savior.

UNIT LESSONS

Lesson 14: **The authority of Jesus**

Lesson 15: **Prayer: The source of power**

Lesson 16: **Jesus' Trial**

Lesson 17: **Jesus' death**

Lesson 18: **Jesus lives!**

Why is this unit necessary?

In these times, many people see Easter as a time for rest or vacation. However, the real meaning of this special celebration is very different.

Religious tradition has also turned everything related to the death and resurrection of Christ into rites and rituals. It is common to see long processions through the main streets of the cities of the world, elaborate rituals that remind us of the painful road leading to Christ's last moments on Calvary.

For Christians, Easter is more than a simple religious celebration. It is the commemoration of the death and resurrection of our Lord and Savior. In addition, it is a time to reflect on the gift of our salvation and give thanks for it.

In this unit, your students will study some events of the life of Jesus, from the triumphal entry to his resurrection. They will learn that prayer is the source of power to face problems. They will also study about the humility and meekness that Jesus had in order to endure the mistreatment, and they will know that through the death of the Son of God, we have life in abundance.

Pray for the Lord to guide you as you prepare these special lessons which will surely impact the lives of your students.

The authority of Jesus

Biblical References: Matthew 21:1-17, 23-27; 26:14-16; 28:18.

Lesson Objective: Preteens learn and accept the authority of Christ in their lives.

Memory Verse: *Jesus said to her, "I am the resurrection and the life. The one who believes in me will live, even though they die; and whoever lives by believing in me will never die.* (John 11:25-26)

PREPARE YOURSELF TO TEACH!

For a large number of people, Jesus was just a historical figure. He is considered a good teacher or a prophet of biblical times. History recognizes him as a master of old times who died at the time of the Roman Empire. However, students must learn that Jesus is the Son of God and has divine authority over our life.

In all interpersonal relationships it is necessary that the parties involved come to know each other more and more, to cement the relationship and create closer links. The same happens in our relationship with the Lord. How can we love Jesus if we do not know him?

Use these lessons so that your students know Jesus Christ more closely, and decide to follow him day by day.

BIBLICAL COMMENTARY

Matthew 21:1-17. The last week that Jesus was on earth, he experienced many emotions: joy, anger, worry and suffering. When he triumphantly arrived in Jerusalem, he affirmed his status as the promised Messiah and the crowd received him as a king. The people, excited to think that he would free them from the suffering and the Roman oppression, threw palm branches on the road for him to pass. The palms were a symbol of prosperity, justice and triumph.

Then he went to the temple, but he did not like what he saw. When people went there to worship, they offered animals as a sacrifice. Many people traveled long distances, so they preferred to buy the animals in the court of the temple. Some travelers came from other countries and had to exchange their foreign currency for local money. But the problem was that the traders and sellers deceived the people to obtain greater profits.

Knowing this, Jesus did not hesitate to drive out the sellers and turn over the tables of the money changers, cleaning the temple of those who exploited the people.

Then the lame and the blind came to him and he healed them.

Later, Jesus confronted the Pharisees who challenged and questioned his authority. They wanted to know by what authority had he thrown the merchants out of the temple and healed the sick.

Jesus, using a common method among the Pharisees, answered them with another question: "Where was John's baptism from? Heaven or men?" (V. 25).

The Pharisees did not know what to answer. They knew that the people would be angry with them if they answered that John's baptism belonged to men, but if they answered that it was from heaven, they would have to recognize Jesus as the Son of God, because John had already prophesied it.

LESSON DEVELOPMENT

Who do you obey?

Place two sheets of paper on the table, and divide the class into two teams. Ask each team to line up as far from the table as possible. Give the first person in each row a marker (make sure it is round or very thick, to avoid accidents).

Tell them that without talking to each other, they must think of the figures who have authority over their lives, that is, those whom they must obey. Then, tell them that the first person of each team should run to the table and write the name of an authority figure. Then he must return running to deliver the marker to the next player, and that person then runs to do the same thing. Continue the game until they can no longer add more names. Allow one member of each team to read their list.

Then ask them:
- How do they feel about having to obey so many people? (Allow them to respond.)
- Did you write the name of Jesus on your lists?
- Why is it important for you to obey Jesus? (Listen to the answers.)

In today's story we will talk about some people who questioned the authority of Jesus.

Who is the authority?

Ask two volunteers to help hand out the student worksheets and pencils.

Then ask the students to find page 53 and discuss what happens when you obey a person with authority.

Allow volunteers to read each of the situations and, together answer the following questions in accordance to each case:
- Who is the authority?
- What do you lose by obeying them?
- What do you gain by obeying them?

BIBLE STORY

If the size of your class allows it, divide your students into four teams and assign them one of the rectangles with questions on page 52. Allow time for them to read the passage and respond. Ask each group to name a representative, who will read the Bible passage and report the team's answer to the other teams.

To conclude, tell them: Through these passages we learned that Jesus has all the authority. Any authority that a person exercises on earth is because He has allowed it. Jesus will judge those who misuse authority or abuse it.

ACTIVITIES

Who is he..?

Ask students to individually complete the activity on page 54. Then, talk about who Jesus is to them. If time allows, encourage them to give a short testimony about their relationship with Jesus.

Read the memory verse on the worksheet a couple of times. Then ask that, without help, they try to repeat it by heart.

Why should I obey?

Write this question on the board and allow time for your students to participate with their answers. Emphasize that, first, we must obey Jesus and his commandments; and then our parents and teachers.

Ask your students to write on a sheet the question and the answers that are on the board. Instruct them to stick it in a visible place in their home, as a reminder that they must obey.

TO FINISH

Make sure students pick up the materials they used before saying goodbye.

Emphasize the importance of remembering Jesus' authority and obeying him. He did not come as a dictator, but as Savior and Redeemer.

Invite your students to evaluate their lives this week, recognizing what areas they need to surrender to Jesus. Give them a few minutes to pray in silence.

Then, conclude by thanking God for sending his only Son. Have a short time of worship before you say goodbye, and encourage them to attend class next week.

Lesson 15

Prayer: the source of power

Biblical References: Luke 22:39-62.

Lesson Objective: That the students learn to follow the example Jesus gave us, and seek strength and security through prayer.

Memory Verse: *Jesus said to her, "I am the resurrection and the life. The one who believes in me will live, even though they die; and whoever lives by believing in me will never die* (John 11:25-26).

PREPARE YOURSELF TO TEACH!

For your students, what their friends say and think about them is very important. They strive to be accepted and belong to the most popular groups. Pre-teens do not want to be different, and they fear that the people they love will abandon them.

Many of them have the support of their family and friends during difficult times, and feel protected. In this lesson, they will learn that although sometimes they will not have the help of anyone and will be alone, God will always be with them. He has provided prayer as a source of power for us to find strength and security.

BIBLICAL COMMENTARY

Luke 22:39-62. On Thursday afternoon, Jesus celebrated the Passover with his disciples and told them that the time of his death was approaching. They did not understand what Jesus anticipated or how close this event was.

At that dinner, Peter confirmed his loyalty to Jesus. However, the Lord knew that Peter had an impulsive temper and that the same night he would deny him three times.

On the Mount of Olives, Jesus left eight disciples at the entrance and called Peter, James and John to pray, while he went away to pray alone. Jesus probably needed the company and support of his friends for the difficult situation he was going to face. But, he knew that he also needed to spend some time in prayer, talking to His heavenly Father.

Jesus' prayer reflected his anguish and fear of the suffering and death that awaited him. Therefore, he asked God to free him from that bitter "cup". But, in spite of what he wanted, Jesus submitted completely to the will of the Father.

The Bible tells us that an angel went to him, giving him the strength to endure the hard ordeal ahead.

On two occasions Jesus told his disciples to pray to not fall into temptation. On both occasions he found them sleeping. They did not realize the importance of their Master's request, and they were not prepared for what would happen hours later. When the priests and soldiers confronted them, they left, leaving Jesus alone.

Prayer was very important for Jesus. He taught us the need to talk to God and tell him about our problems and sufferings. That night in the garden, he asked his disciples to pray and, even today, he reminds us that prayer is our source of power.

LESSON DEVELOPMENT

I feel so alone!

For this activity we suggest that you write the following cases on several cards. Ask that three pairs of volunteers who agree to do a skit, come forward and take one of the cards.

The couple must present, in front of the group, the case described on the card. Give five minutes for the participants to choose the characters they will present.

1. Mariana offered Sofia a cigarette. When she did not accept, Mariana mocked her and threatened her by telling her that she would convince all the girls in the class not to talk to her. Now Sofia feels very lonely and thinks that she no longer has friends.

2. Gonzalo is sick, and the doctor told him that he could not leave his house for two weeks. His friend Mauricio went to visit him, and told him that he and all the other children in the neighborhood were going to a summer camp for two weeks. Gonzalo feels that now that he is sick, all his friends have abandoned him.

3. Alejandra and Victoria were friends for a long time. Victoria's parents decided that they would move to another city. When it was time to say goodbye, Alejandra became very sad. Victoria also cried because she thinks she will not find another friend

Tell them that on many occasions, we go through difficult times and feel that everyone has abandoned us. In today's class, we will talk about what Jesus did the day he felt the most sad and lonely.

Investigation

For this activity you will need several Bibles that have a concordance. Divide the students into small groups, according to the number of Bibles you have on hand.

Ask them to look for at least ten passages that contain the words: pray, prayer, prayers, praying, etc. and read the biblical quote and take notes to share with the class.

Tell them: The Bible teaches us a lot about prayer. Jesus told his disciples that they should pray. Through the Lord's Prayer, he taught us how to do it. In today's Bible story, we will study what Jesus did on a very sad night.

BIBLE STORY

Make a brief introduction before beginning the Bible story (for example: Jesus had come to Jerusalem and decided to celebrate the Passover with his disciples. Then, knowing that the moment of his death was approaching, he decided to go to a garden to talk with God).

Once again, divide the class into small groups, and assign them some of the questions on page 55 of the worksheet. Allow time for each team to search for the Bible passage and answer the corresponding questions.

A volunteer from each team should read the answers aloud, or write them on the board so that everyone can write them down on their worksheets.

Make clarifications, and reinforce your students answers with today's passage.

ACTIVITIES

The source of power

Ask the students to find page 56 on their worksheet while you write the word "PRAYER" on the board. Ask seven students to look up the biblical passages and read them. Then, decide which of these verses talks about the importance of prayer in the lives of preadolescents.

Write the answers on the board, and give time for them to write them down on their worksheets.

- Jeremiah 42:3 - Through prayer we can ask God to guide us.
- Matthew 5:44 - We should pray for those who persecute us.
- Luke 6:28 - We should pray for those who mistreat us.
- Luke 22:40 - Prayer gives us strength to resist temptation.
- James 5:13-14 - We can pray when we are sick or have problems.

Which should I use?

Discuss the types of prayer mentioned on page 57 of the worksheet. Then, connect the prayers on the right with the types of prayers found in the graphic.

To conclude the activity, tell them: Some people like to say long prayers with very complicated words, and it's not bad, but that does not mean that God will pay more attention. God listens to all those who pray with a sincere heart and wish to please Him.

When we spend time in prayer, we can learn more from God and get closer to him.

My source of strength and power

Provide scissors for your students to cut page 58 of the book and fold it to form a prayer book.

Explain that in that booklet they should write their prayer requests every day and the answers they receive. Emphasize that prayer is not to present our list of requests to God, but to have a time of communion with him.

Encourage your students to keep the prayer book in their Bible and to use it during their devotional time.

TO FINISH

Ask that two volunteers intercede for the requests that the members of the group have brought.

Conclude by thanking God for giving us prayer as a source of power and strength.

Invite them to next week's class, and do not forget to contact those who are sick or absent for other reasons.

Lesson 16
Jesus' Trial

Biblical References: Matthew 27:11-26; Mark 14:53-63; Luke 23:4-12; John18:12; 19:16.

Lesson objective: For students to stand firm in their faith, despite persecution.

Memory Verse: *Jesus said to her, "I am the resurrection and the life. The one who believes in me will live, even though they die; and whoever lives by believing in me will never die.* (John 11:25-26)

PREPARE YOURSELF TO TEACH!

One of the characteristics of most preadolescents is that they are perseverate. When they believe in something or make a decision, they defend it with intensity. Today's lesson will make them aware of the perseverance of Jesus, who remained firm even in the midst of the most terrible persecution.

The story of Jesus' unjust judgment will help them understand that, even if they face opposition and danger, if they remain steadfast in their faith in God, he will help them emerge victorious.

Take advantage of the perseverance of your students to encourage them to defend their faith with love and wisdom before those who question them.

BIBLICAL COMMENTARY

John 18:12; 19:16. In a matter of hours, Jesus was arrested and brought before Annas, Caiaphas, Pilate, and Herod, and sentenced to death. They may have taken him to Annas during the night. This violated Jewish religious laws, and showed the urgency of the Pharisees, priests and leaders to condemn him.

Although Jesus was innocent, the Sanhedrin used the testimony of false witnesses to indict him and subjected him to an illegal trial. They accused him of blasphemy for saying he was the Son of God. According to Roman laws, blasphemy was not punishable by the death penalty. However, the temple leaders also accused him of treason, which justified his death on the cross.

When Jesus was facing Pilate, the governor showed some degree of respect for him, and was convinced of his innocence. Again and again he told the people that he did not find a reason to punish him. Hoping to satisfy the crowd who wanted to see Jesus dead, he ordered that they beat him. He thought that after that punishment he could let him go free. But it was not like that. Although they saw Jesus tortured and suffer, the Jewish people and leaders would not be satisfied until they saw him on the cross.

All of Pilate's attempts were futile. When the chief priest accused him of going against Caesar, Pilate surrendered Jesus into the hands of the enraged multitude for fear of losing his position.

LESSON DEVELOPMENT

Who was Pilate?

Without saying the name of the character, tell your students the following biography:

This man was the Roman governor of the province of Judea (26-36 AD). He is famous for his intervention in the judgment and execution of Jesus Christ.

As governor of Judea, he had absolute authority over all citizens who were not Romans. But in many cases, especially those related to religion, they were judged by the Sanhedrin, which was the council and supreme court of the Jews. After this court decided that Jesus Christ was guilty of blasphemy, they sent Jesus to the Roman court, because they could not dictate a death sentence.

When the governor refused to condemn him to death, the Jewish priests presented other false accusations against Jesus. Then the governor interrogated him alone. Impressed by the dignity and frankness of Jesus' answers, he tried to save him (John 18:38-39; 19:12-15), but the fear of a Jewish uprising finally made him accept the demands of the people. Therefore, Jesus was crucified.

Ask them: What is this character's name? Listen to answers and congratulate those who answer correctly. Tell them that in today's story they will study about the judgment made against Jesus in front of this Roman governor.

Persecution

Write on the chalkboard the word "persecution" and its definition. Ask your class to give some examples of persecution suffered by Christians around the world. (For example, in certain countries Christians cannot congregate, and if they do they are imprisoned. In some rural areas, Christians are expelled from the community because of their faith.) Tell them that in today's story, they will learn from a man who endured persecution and remained firm until the end.

BIBLE STORY

Hand out the student worksheets, and direct them to page 60.

Choose several students to dramatize the suggested theater script. Each one will represent a character, changing their voice so that it is as real as possible. If you have tunics or costumes, they can wear them, and organize a small stage performance.

While your students read or dramatize the script, ask them to pay close attention to the way the crowd treated Jesus.

Then ask them: How did Jesus respond to the accusations? How do you think he felt while all this was happening?

ACTIVITIES

A true story

Have your students sit in a circle, and tell them the following story.

Li Ying was a young girl when she decided to do the church's work. From the day she accepted Christ in her heart, she knew that the path would not be easy, especially since she lived in China, a country in which Christianity is forbidden. When she entered university, Li Ying decided to study journalism. After many years of study, she graduated and started working. However, she knew that she should use her talent for God's work. Therefore, although the authorities prohibited it, she decided to publish a Christian magazine. Soon after starting the printing and distribution of the magazine, Li Ying was arrested for violating Chinese laws, and now serves a sentence of 15 years in prison. Part of her punishment is to remain completely silent. She cannot say a single word to her fellow prisoners. In addition, she has to work 16 hours a day, making handicrafts that are then sold in tourist markets.

Invite your students to reflect on this story, and help them understand that Christian persecution is much more serious and more frequent than they imagine. (For more information on this and other stories of persecuted Christians, visit the page www.persecution.com or www.christianpersecution.com - Both websites belong to the Christian organization "The voice of the martyrs.")

Letters to Li Ying

Provide them with paper and pencils so they can write something they would like to say to Li Ying. When they are finished, place all the letters in a basket or on the table, and form a circle to intercede for this sister who is suffering only because she believes in Christ.

Invite them to remember Li Ying in their daily prayers, as well as thousands of Christians who, like her, suffer every day because of their faith.

To Finish

Repeat the memory verse several times and conclude by singing songs of praise. Remind them that in the next class they will study the lesson about Jesus' death. Encourage them to attend on time.

Jesus' Death

Biblical References: Matthew 27:32-66.

Lesson Objective: Students learn that Jesus died for them.

Memory Verse: *Jesus said to her, "I am the resurrection and the life. The one who believes in me will live, even though they die; and whoever lives by believing in me will never die.* (John 11:25-26)

PREPARE YOURSELF TO TEACH!

In general, preteens recognize when they do something wrong. Children who grew up in Christian homes know that they should ask for forgiveness when they deliberately disobey God.

On the other hand, those who grew up in non-Christian families know the difference between good and the bad, and know that their conscience will alert them when they do the wrong thing.

In addition, all children know that sooner or later, disobedience and misconduct bring consequences, since they have already experienced this. For example, they know that they will receive punishment if they hurt their younger brother or if they disrespect an adult.

Everyone should understand that through the death of Jesus, they can receive forgiveness for their sins. This lesson will help them understand that the suffering and death of Jesus Christ is the price of our salvation.

BIBLICAL COMMENTARY

Matthew 27:32-66. The persecution of Jesus did not end with an unfair trial. On the way to Calvary, the Jewish leaders went by Jesus' side, mocking and challenging him to show his power and save himself. The blows and lashes had weakened him in such a way that he could not carry the weight of the cross.

Then they ordered a man from Cyrene to help the Savior carry the heavy cross. Historians say that the cross weighed between 34 and 56 kg (75 to 125 pounds).

Jesus felt like his Father had forsaken him. Sin separates people from God, and on this sad occasion, Jesus bore the sins of the whole world.

The only ones who remained faithful to Jesus were the women who accompanied him at the foot of the cross during the whole time of his agony.

Joseph of Arimathea showed great courage by appearing before Pilate to ask for Jesus' body in order to bury him. Joseph and Nicodemus took the body and, wrapping it in canvas with spices, they placed it in a grave that was in a garden.

The Jewish leaders tried to make Jesus feel like the worst of criminals, sentencing him to a death destined for the most terrible people. However, Joseph of Arimathea and Nicodemus honored the Master, placing his body in a new tomb and wrapping it in a sheet perfumed with costly aromatic spices.

At the moment Jesus died, the veil of the temple was torn in half, giving us direct access to God. Now we can worship God anywhere and at any time. The death of Jesus provided a bridge to restore our relationship with God and give us eternal life.

LESSON DEVELOPMENT

Welcome your students, and start the class by singing some praises. We suggest that you briefly review the previous lessons before starting the study today, especially if new students are present.

Memory Verse Activity

To review the memory verse, ask the class to look for the words hidden and mixed up in the puzzle on page 66 of the student worksheet.

Then, repeat the verse together, and help those who have difficulty learning it.

Why did the Romans crucify criminals?

Last week we saw that Jesus was sentenced to die on a cross. However, it is likely that your students do not understand what that means in its entirety.

Explain that crucifixion was a form of execution, which consisted in binding or nailing the victim to a cross. This death penalty was common from the 6th century B.C. until the 4th century A.D, especially among the Persians, Egyptians, Romans and Carthaginians. The Romans used it to execute the slaves and criminals; they never used it on their own citizens. The Roman laws specified that the condemned should be flogged.

Jesus had to carry the cross from the point where he had been subjected to torture to the place of execution. Today's story tells us about that sad day when Jesus was nailed to a cross.

What would you sacrifice for your sins?

Ask your students to turn to page 63 in their worksheets. Use this activity to give a brief explanation of the sacrificial system used in the Old Testament.

Tell them: In the time of the Old Testament, people offered sacrifices to express gratitude to God or to ask for forgiveness for their sins. The first sacrificed animal was to atone for the sins of Adam and Eve. Although grain offerings were also presented, the common sacrifice was animals.

The prophets warned the people that their sacrifices were not enough if they did not love and obey God. The sacrifices of the Old Testament were a sign of the way Jesus was going to die.

The theme of today's class refers to the last sacrifice that was offered on earth for the forgiveness of our sins: the death of Jesus.

Build an altar

For this activity you will need several medium-sized stones. Have students form a circle, and give one stone to each one. Ask them to use the stones to build an altar, arranging the stones one on the other. Then, place some wooden sticks on top.

Tell them: Long ago, people built altars similar to this one to offer sacrifices to God. What would you sacrifice to God to show him that you are sorry for all the wrong you have done? (Allow them to respond). What would you offer to express your gratitude and love for having your sins forgiven?

Tell them that in today's story they will learn that we do not need to offer more sacrifices, because God provided another means for the forgiveness of sins.

BIBLE STORY

Ask a member of your congregation to dress in a tunic and represent a biblical messenger, giving the following information:

Last minute news: Jesus of Nazareth was condemned to die! Pilate was the one who gave the order. After beating and whipping him, the Roman court declared Jesus Christ guilty of treason, and within a few hours he will be executed.

The condemned man will have to carry his cross of around 50 kg. up to Golgotha (place of the Skull), where he will be crucified.

A large crowd has gathered near the place of execution to witness the event. If you want to know more details of this story, read our informative section in Matthew 27:32-66.

Thank the visitor for their participation. Then, ask everyone to take turns reading aloud the passage from Matthew.

ACTIVITIES

Why did Jesus have to die?

Have the students find pages 64 and 65 in their worksheets. Divide the class into pairs or small groups, and instruct them to help each other find the Bible verses and then the missing words. Then, talk about the importance of Jesus' death and its meaning for all Christians around the world.

The plan of salvation

For this activity you will need five cardboard hearts of the following colors: dark, red, white and yellow.

Stick the hearts on the board in the order mentioned, and use them to explain the plan of salvation to the preadolescents. Remember that the most important thing is to pray for the Holy Spirit to touch the hearts of your students.

The dark heart represents the sin that exists in us and that separates us from God. When there is sin in our hearts, we cannot have a relationship with God and we live in darkness.

The red heart represents the blood that Christ shed on the cross of Calvary to give us salvation. Through the sacrifice of Jesus, our sins are erased and our relationship with God the Father is restored.

The white heart represents the cleansing that Jesus Christ does in our life. He removes all the bad things that used to be in us and makes us "new creatures".

The yellow heart represents eternal life. Jesus Christ promised us that we will go to live with him in the heavenly mansions, where the streets are golden and there is a "clean river of water of life as splendid as crystal" (Revelation 21:21b; 22:1).

Explain to your students that accepting Christ in their hearts is the most important decision of their lives. Ask if some wish to make that decision. If so, lead them in prayer. (Do not forget to start discipling those who accepted the invitation, and encourage them to live the Christian life.)

TO FINISH

Congratulate those who received Christ and tell them that they are now part of the family of God.

To end, worship and give thanks to God for having sent his Son Jesus to die for us.

It is important that you maintain weekly contact with your students. If possible, visit them or call them by phone, and do not forget to invite them to the next class to study the resurrection of Jesus.

notes

Lesson 18

Jesus Lives!

Biblical References: Matthew 28:1-20.

Lesson objective: That the students learn that Jesus was resurrected from the dead.

Memory Verse: *Jesus said to her, "I am the resurrection and the life. The one who believes in me will live, even though they die; 26 and whoever lives by believing in me will never die. (John 11:25-26)*

PREPARE YOURSELF TO TEACH!

It is likely that some of your students have not yet experienced the death of a relative or close friend. However, most know that losing a loved one is a painful experience.

Today's lesson not only tells us about the suffering of the disciples and the women who followed Jesus, but also about the joy they felt when they learned that their Lord had conquered death and was alive.

A distinctive feature of the Christian faith is that our leader lives, while the leaders of other religions died a long time ago. God raised Jesus from the grave. Now he is seated at the right hand of the Father, ready to help Christians live happy, victorious, and full of hope.

Tell your students about your joy of knowing that we believe in a living God who did not stay in the grave, but rose from the dead and will soon return for his people.

BIBLICAL COMMENTARY

Matthew 28:1-20. Very early in the morning, before the sun came out on the first day of the week, the story began a new chapter. For the women who went to the grave, everything changed. Upon learning their Master was alive, the suffering because of the death of Jesus became an indescribable joy.

The angel gave news of joy and hope, not only for those women and disciples, but for all who now believe in him.

These women received a great reward for their faithfulness during the crucifixion of Jesus: they were the first to know and tell the good news to the disciples.

However, they were not the only ones who spoke about the resurrection of Jesus. The soldiers reported the event to their superiors. After a quick meeting, the Sanhedrin agreed to offer them money to tell them that the disciples had stolen Jesus' body while they slept.

For Roman soldiers, sleeping during work time was a crime punishable by death. However, the religious leaders promised to intercede for them with the government officials if a problem arose. In addition, they were offered a large amount of money if they spread the rumor about the theft of Jesus' body.

But that did not intimidate the disciples. From that moment, they announced the good news of the Resurrection of the Savior.

LESSON DEVELOPMENT

Receive your students with joy, and tell them that in today's class, you will tell them Good News. After praying to start the class, ask that some volunteers briefly tell what they learned about Jesus in the previous lessons.

Tombs or cemeteries?

Explain to your students the difference between the cemeteries we know now and the tombs of the Old Testament. Tell them that the custom of Bible times was to prepare the body of the deceased with aromatic herbs, such as myrrh and aloe, for its preservation. Then, they would wrap it in cloth and place it in a tomb carved in a rock or stone.

Jesus' tomb was special because it was new and in a garden. After placing the Master's body there, they sealed the entrance with a very large stone to prevent anyone from entering.

BIBLE STORY

Distribute the student's worksheets and direct them to page 68. Allow time for the students to organize into teams and choose the characters from the Bible story they want to represent.

If you wish, ask them to dramatize the story, or just read the script, changing their voice to make it more real. If your class is large, divide it into two groups. One will represent the biblical story first and the other will be the audience. Then they will exchange places so that everyone participates.

If possible, get robes or costumes. If your students feel sufficiently prepared, invite other small children to see the drama.

ACTIVITIES

Newspaper Mural

For this activity you will need cardboard, white paper, colored pencils, scissors, glue and other decorating materials.

Place all the materials on a table for the students to make a mural about the story of the resurrection. Stay close to make suggestions or provide help to those who need it.

They can make individual drawings and then paste them on a single card, or make a single drawing in which everyone participates. Do not forget to write the memory verse as the title of the mural. Then you can place it in some visible place.

Messenger Rocks

During the week, get a small smooth stone for each member of your class. You will also need markers.

Give the materials to your students and ask them to write on their stone: JESUS LIVES! Then, let them decorate it with the markers. Tell them that it will serve as a reminder of Jesus' victory over death and what he represents for them as Christians.

General Review

Give the children a soft ball or object so that they can pass it from hand to hand, while they listen to a melody. When the music stops, whoever has the object in their hand should say something they learned during this series of lessons (for example: the name of the Roman governor who judged Jesus, the animal on which Jesus rode when entering Jerusalem, etc.).

Continue the game until everyone has participated at least once.

TO FINISH

Ask those who learned the memory verse to come forward and say it out loud. We suggest that you reward their effort with a simple gift (for example: a pencil or a candy).

Form a circle, and ask for three volunteers who wish to pray. The first must pray for the requests. The second will give thanks to God for the lesson, and the third will intercede for the students who did not attend the class.

Thank them for their attendance throughout the unit. If possible, make certificates for attendance and participation for those who did not miss during the past weeks. That will motivate them to remain faithful in attendance.

Invite them to the next class to begin Unit IV, "God helps you," and say goodbye by singing a song about the risen Lord.

GOD HELPS YOU

Biblical References: Joshua 10:1-21; Judges 13:1-25; 14:1-20; 15:1-17; 16:4-31.

Unit verse: *Trust in the Lord with all your heart and lean not on your own understanding; in all your ways submit to him, and he will make your paths straight* (Proverbs 3:5-6).

The purpose of this unit
This unit will help preteens to:

- Recognize the sovereignty of God and trust in his protection - even if they do not understand what is happening around them.

- Decide to follow God to avoid sin and its consequences.

Unit Lessons

Lesson 19: God is in control

Lesson 20: A good start for Samson

Lesson 21: A very strong man

Lesson 22: A great loss

Why do preteens need this lesson?

In this unit your students will study what two Old Testament characters, Joshua and Samson, experienced and the decisions they made. Through the development of these lessons, they will understand that God is sovereign.

Highlight divine sovereignty; emphasize the memory verse (Proverbs 3:5-6) and each lesson activity.

By knowing the decisions they made, as well as the actions and consequences that occurred in the lives of these characters, students will learn that God is in control of all situations. However, he allows us to freely make decisions, and afterwards we enjoy or suffer the consequences.

When young people face difficult times and suffering, they are likely to wonder why it happens to them. Maybe God will not reveal the answer, but they will remember that he promised to help them resist and overcome if they trust him.

Lesson 19
God is in control

Biblical References: Joshua 10:1-21

Lesson objective: That the students learn that God is sovereign.

Memory Verse: *Trust in the Lord with all your heart and lean not on your own understanding; in all your ways submit to him, and he will make your paths straight* (Proverbs 3:5-6).

PREPARE YOURSELF TO TEACH!

Preteens are leaving behind the stability of childhood to enter a stage of rapid changes in their life. It is likely that this transition will disorient and confuse them and even cause pain. They need a solid anchor in their life. They must learn that although the situation is difficult and painful, God is sovereign and almighty.

It is also important that they understand that God intervenes to order our life. Maybe he does it silently, almost without us noticing, or with miraculous demonstrations of his power. In whatever form, God is in control of the whole world, and even the most powerful forces in nature obey Him. As the sovereign Lord of the universe, God deserves our loyalty, love and obedience.

BIBLICAL COMMENTARY

Joshua 10:1-21. The Israelites had a significant military presence in Canaan. They had defeated Jericho and other neighboring towns. Those of Gibeon managed to trick Joshua into signing a peace treaty (Joshua 9). When the other nations heard about it, they joined together to punish Gibeon.

Although the Gibeonites had deceived Joshua, he kept his promise and helped them. The army of Israel, which was relatively new, had to fight against the armies of five great cities at once: Jerusalem, Hebron, Jarmuth, Lachish and Eglon. The Israelites hoped to take the cities one by one, as they did with Jericho, but the plan did not work.

Although their plans failed, God promised Joshua victory. And he showed his sovereignty over the armies, confusing the enemies when Joshua attacked them. In addition, he showed His sovereignty over nature, sending a storm of hail that destroyed the enemy armies. He also demonstrated his sovereignty over time by answering Joshua's prayer and stopping the orbit of the moon and the sun. And last, he showed his sovereignty over other gods, giving his people the victory over the pagan armies.

LESSON DEVELOPMENT

God did it

Start the class by asking your students: Do you remember any time in your life when you wanted a miracle to occur? Allow some volunteers to respond, or ask them directly by name. Emphasize that miracles show that God is in control of the situation.

Ask them to find worksheet page 69. Divide the class into small groups to work on the alphabet soup. Gather your students and compare the words they found. They are: LAZARUS, CARMEL, INVISIBLE, ELISHA, RED, HEALED, FISH, GOD, JORDAN.

Remind them that God is sovereign; therefore, He has the power to perform miracles. Miracles are a way in which God shows his sovereignty over nature and lives of people. If time allows, review what miracles God did in each of the stories represented in the alphabet soup. In what ways did God show his sovereignty?

BIBLE STORY

5 cities against a sovereign God

Read together the passage from Joshua 10:1-21. As you read, ask the students to identify the various ways in which God demonstrated his sovereignty in each situation. To encourage discussion, use the following questions:

- How did God show that he was in control of the situation? (v. 8) (God told Joshua that the enemy would not defeat Israel. In addition, he confused the enemy army, sending a storm of hail to attack them. This favored the triumph of Joshua and the Israelites.)

- Why did God encourage Joshua before he fought against the enemy? (The Israelite army did not compare with the army of the five enemy cities. God wanted to assure Joshua that He would accompany them and that the Hebrew army would triumph in battle with the help of the Almighty.)

God, our help in any trouble

Joshua and the Israelites recognized that God was sovereign. This recognition made the difference when confronting enemies.

It is important to understand that the sovereignty of God is not limited by the lack of understanding of man.

Read Joshua 10:19 and reflect on the victory that God gave the Israelites, even though they faced a very large army. Neither the size of the army, nor the power of their weapons, nor time limited God.

Divide the class into small groups to answer the questions in the worksheet, page 71. Then, discuss the answers.

1. Why did Joshua help the people of Gibeon?

   (The combined forces of the Amorite kings would attack Gibeon. The Israelites had made a deal with the Gibeonites. Although they lied in making the deal, Joshua felt he had to do his part and help them in the battle.)

2. Why did God send hail?

   (He used his sovereignty over nature to help his people in a time of need.)

3. God does not always use miracles to fulfill his plans. What do you think about that?

Our Amazing God

Divide the class into pairs or small groups to work on the next activity on page 71. Each group should choose a secretary to write down the answers.

- What does sovereignty mean?

   (God has the absolute right to rule over the entire universe and everything that exists or He wants to add, in the way he sees fit, with no limits imposed by circumstances or human decisions.)

- How does the sovereignty of God help us?

   (God has control of the entire world. No matter how difficult the circumstances may be, God has everything under his dominion.)

- Sometimes kings and queens are called "sovereigns" because they have control over their countries. Since God is sovereign, how should we relate to him?

   (We must respect him as he deserves, honor his name, follow his teachings, be obedient, be reverent when we are in the church sanctuary and when we participate in the times of worship and communion.)

TO FINISH

How do you feel?

Allow time for your students to go to page 72, and observe the expression of the characters' faces. Ask them to circle the feelings they have when they think about God's sovereignty. (Possible answers: happy, ashamed, sad, amazed, excited, strong, confused, frightened, proud). Ask volunteers to tell and explain their answers.

It is important to emphasize that sovereignty without love can be cruel and painful. There is an old saying that says: "Power corrupts and absolute power corrupts absolutely." However, we should not be afraid of God. Although he is sovereign and powerful, he also loves us.

The sovereign God of the universe invites us to love and follow him.

Personal Reflection

This is a good time for the group to reflect on some personal aspects related to the sovereignty of God in their lives.

- Do I allow God to control my life, or do I try to do it myself?

- Am I worried about situations that I am sure God has under his control? Why?

Encourage them to leave all their fears and concerns in God's hands.

Review the memory verse, and finally, ask that a member of the class finish with prayer. Do not forget to invite them to the next class.

A good start for Samson

Biblical References: Judges 13:1-25.

Lesson Objective: That the students learn what it means to live a holy life.

Memory Verse: *Trust in the Lord with all your heart and lean not on your own understanding; in all your ways submit to him, and he will make your paths straight* (Proverbs 3:5-6).

PREPARE YOURSELF TO TEACH!

As we know, the world we live in is corrupted by sin. Television, radio and other media promote immoral actions and lifestyles. Likewise, preadolescents feel pressure from their friends to do what is wrong.

Surely they've characters that they admire - even famous athletes - who have been arrested for driving drunk, consuming or having drugs, or performing immoral acts. When observing such conduct, many young people come to consider it acceptable.

However, God asks us to have a different lifestyle: holiness. It is true that people who live in holiness do not constitute the majority, but preadolescents must understand what God demands: that His children do not conform to the ways of this world, but that they live in holiness.

God gave Samson a special mission to help his people. That is why he gave him a series of requirements that he had to fulfill.

Also, Christian pre-teens have the responsibility to live according to the commands of the Lord. And, just as God was with Samson, he promised that he would be with us, helping us to live in holiness.

BIBLICAL COMMENTARY

Judges 13:1-25. The Philistines, a warrior people established in the coastal plain of Palestine, left their five main cities to attack the Israelites and Canaanites. They were more powerful than the other people thanks to their chariots, iron swords and spears.

One day, an angel appeared to Samson's mother to tell her that she would have a son. As a sign of God's promise, they should not cut off his hair, he could not drink wine or eat the fruit of the vine, nor touch corpses. God's plan for Samson was to free the Israelites from the Philistine attacks.

1 Peter 1:15. God wants to use his children for his service; thus, he establishes rules of conduct that we must comply with. He asks for our obedience and holiness. That does not mean that we must be as holy as he is, because we are human beings, but that we must have his character, which is holy, because we were made in his image. Just as a glass filled with ocean water has the same properties as the ocean, human beings must have the purity and holiness of God.

Our lifestyle and conversation should reflect such holiness. What is in the heart shows itself in every aspect of life. In the Old Testament, holiness included rites and ceremonies, but in the New Testament, holiness is an integral part of daily life. God calls us to be holy ones (saints) and live an integral life that reflects the change he has made in us.

LESSON DEVELOPMENT

Who was Samson?

On a blackboard or on a large piece of paper, write as a title: "Samson." Then, ask your students to call out the facts they know about this man: names of his parents, place of birth, occupation, characteristics, where he lived, whether he was married or single, etc.

Write on the board the information they give you. If possible, provide biblical dictionaries, encyclopedias, or Bible commentaries, and encourage them to discover as much information about Samson as they can.

Review

It is important to verify if your students understood what God's sovereignty means in their lives. Ask questions that help reinforce learning, such as: What situations did you experience last week that made you less worried because you trusted God more?

What do you think?

Allow time for your students to read the statements in the work sheet individually (page 73). Then, read them all together by following these instructions:

If you agree with the corresponding statement, stand up while we read it.

If you do not agree, read it sitting down.

Take note of how many agree and how many disagree, but avoid making comments. At the end of the lesson, repeat the activity and see if they change their minds.

Declarations:

1. As a Christian, I am free to do what I want.
2. As a Christian, I must apologize if I sin.
3. God does not care how I live.
4. The Bible has such high demands that people find it difficult to fulfill them.
5. Through the Holy Spirit, God empowers us to live in holiness.
6. God wants us to live in holiness.

BIBLE STORY

Samson and John the Baptist

Use this activity to compare the lives of two Nazarites: Samson, of the Old Testament, and John the Baptist, of the New.

Old Testament: The neighboring peoples of the Israelites worshiped false gods. Many Israelite children when they grew up wanted to imitate them. They made images, put them in their courtyards and bowed before them to worship them.

As people turned away from God, he allowed them to have problems. In the coastal area lived the Philistines, who were cruel and strong. For 40 years they dominated the tribes of Israel that lived nearby. The Philistines worshiped the god Dagon. This idol had a man's face and hands, and the body of a fish. The Philistines built a great temple for Dagon in their capital city.

However, not all Israelites worshiped false gods. Some loved and served God. Among them was Manoa and his wife, an elderly couple who had no children.

One day, an angel told Manoa's wife: "You are barren and childless, but you are going to become pregnant and give birth to a son. Now see to it that you drink no wine or other fermented drink and that you do not eat anything unclean. You will become pregnant and have a son whose head is never to be touched by a razor because the boy is to be a Nazirite, dedicated to God from the womb. He will take the lead in delivering Israel from the hands of the Philistines. "

When she told Manoa about this, he prayed, "Pardon your servant, Lord. I beg you to let the man of God you sent to us come again to teach us how to bring up the boy who is to be born."

God heard Manoah and when his wife was out in the field, the angel returned, so she ran to call her husband. Manoah asked the angel, "When your words are fulfilled, what is to be the rule that governs the boy's life and work?"

The angel replied, "Your wife must do all that I have told her."

Then Manoah and his wife offered a sacrifice to God. When the flame ascended from the altar to heaven, Manoah and his wife saw the angel of the Lord rise in the flame.

After a while, Manoah's wife gave birth to a son and named him Samson. His parents raised him according to the Nazirite vows. They never cut his hair; they did not allow him to eat unclean food or drink any kind of wine. These were some of the restrictions that the Nazirites had to fulfill. Samson grew strong and God blessed him. (Judges 13:2-24)

Important fact: "Samson must be a Nazirite." A Nazirite was a person who, by means of a vow, was set apart for the service of God. Samson's parents made the vow for him. Sometimes this was temporary, but in the case of Samson, it was for life" (Daily Living Bible).

The New Testament tells us about another Nazirite man.

Zechariah had left his home in the mountains to fulfill his time of service as a priest in the temple. Since there were many priests, they took turns ministering.

Zechariah and his wife Elizabeth loved and served God, and awaited the coming of the Messiah, but they had no children.

Twice a day Zechariah would take burning coals from the altar and take them to the sanctuary to offer incense to God. One day when entering the sanctuary, Zechariah saw an angel and was afraid.

The angel said to him, "Do not be afraid, Zechariah; your prayer has been heard. Your wife Elizabeth will bear you a son, and you are to call him John. He will be a joy and delight to you, and many will rejoice because of his birth, for he will be great in the sight of the Lord. He is never to take wine or other fermented drink, and he will be filled with the Holy Spirit even before he is born. He will bring back many of the people of Israel to the Lord their God. And he will go on before the Lord, in the spirit and power of Elijah, to turn the hearts of the parents to their children and the disobedient to the wisdom of the righteous—to make ready a people prepared for the Lord."

It seemed incredible to Zechariah what the angel was saying, so he asked, "How will I know this? Because I am old and my wife is old."

The angel replied, "I am Gabriel. I stand in the presence of God, and I have been sent to speak to you and to tell you this good news. And now you will be silent and not able to speak until the day this happens, because you did not believe my words."

Those who were in the courtyard of the temple wondered why Zechariah took so long in the sanctuary. When, at last, he came out, he could not speak. He communicated by making signs. Then they realized that he had seen a vision. When he completed his ministry, he went home. Later, his wife, Elizabeth, conceived and gave birth to a boy.

According to Jewish custom, the father named his son eight days after birth. That day, relatives and friends arrived, hoping that the boy would take his father's name.

When Elizabeth announced that the baby would be called John they all looked at Zechariah to see his reaction. But he wrote on a tablet: "His name is John." Immediately he regained his speech and praised God. Then, he prophesied that his son would go before the Lord to prepare the way. John would teach the people that they could be saved if they repented of their sins.

He grew big and strong. And when he was almost 30 years old, he left home and began to preach next to the Jordan River. People from all over came to hear him, and he baptized those who repented of their sins. One day, John had the privilege of baptizing Jesus. Because he baptized people, they called him John the Baptist. (Luke 1:13-24, 57).

Same or different?

Compare, along with your students, the life of Samson with that of John the Baptist. Divide the board into two columns. In one column write the similarities, and in the other the differences. See the examples below:

Similarities: Their parents had no children; the birth of both of them was special; God set them apart for a special purpose; They were Nazarites, etc.

Differences: They lived in different periods; John faced opposition from religious leaders; Samson faced the opposition of the Philistines. Samson saved the people from the oppression of the Philistines; John preached to people about repentance.

Let's Reflect

Before class, prepare a poster with the image of a person who represents a "saint" or who has a halo on his head. Ask the group: Why do we say that this person is holy?

Usually, preteens think that holiness is unattainable or that it is only for the elderly. It is important to emphasize that the holy life goes beyond a posture or conduct in church. We can pretend that we are saints while we are at church or in front of others, but the holy life is demonstrated in daily life, in dealing with people.

Emphasize that selfishness, dishonesty, injustice, lies, disobedience, envy, hypocrisy, ill-intentioned comments, indifference to the need of the sufferer, abuse, jokes, words of double meaning, etc., are not characteristic of a person who lives in holiness.

Ask them: Is it possible for a boy or girl their age in the 21st century to live a holy life? How can you live according to what God wants for you?

Read 1 Peter 1:15. Remind them that holy life implies: sharing what we have with others; being compassionate to the needs of others; being obedient to God and parents; being honest in the use of time and money; always speaking the truth; avoiding gossip; being respectful and fair in dealing with others. Encourage them to find friends who support them in reading the Bible daily, and participating in times of worship as a family or at church.

The hardest part

Divide the class into small groups. Ask them, using the student activity sheet (page 76), to make a list of areas where it is harder for them to submit to God's will, either because of peer pressure, or because that behavior is common in the group or community where they live. Encourage them to ask for God's help to live in holiness and resist temptation.

TO FINISH

Conclude the class by reading the statements in the student worksheet again found on page 73 and see if they've changed their opinions. Then, pray for each one and ask the Lord to help them live according to 1 Peter 1:15.

Repeat the memory verse together.

notes

Lesson 21

A very strong man

Biblical References: Judges 14:1-20; 15:1-17.

Lesson objective: That the students learn that their relationship with God implies responsibilities.

Memory Verse: *Trust in the Lord with all your heart and lean not on your own understanding; in all your ways submit to him, and he will make your paths straight* (Proverbs 3:5-6).

PREPARE YOURSELF TO TEACH!

When preadolescents face an unstable friendship, they often decide that it is not worth keeping. They are learning that establishing and cultivating a good friendship demands effort. If only one person gives, without receiving anything from the other, that relationship will not last.

This example will help them understand that the relationship between God and his people must be mutual. God expects obedience and faithfulness from his people in response to the genuine love he shows us. Both parties must work towards that goal to maintain the relationship. God made a covenant with Samson. And even though Samson did not always behave correctly, God fulfilled his part of the covenant and worked through an imperfect Samson to carry out his plan.

Young people will be encouraged to know that they do not need to be perfect to have a relationship with God. However, they must meet the requirements to maintain it.

BIBLICAL COMMENTARY

Judges 14:1-20; 15:1-20. These two chapters on Samson's life are complex, a combination of comedy and tragedy. Samson showed humility and pride at the same time. He was stubborn, but he recognized that his strength came from God. We see an incredible strength in Samson, but he was lacking in discipline and let himself get carried away by his emotions. The most important thing in this story is that it shows God's faithfulness and willingness to use an imperfect servant to carry out his divine plan.

From the beginning, we see a stubborn Samson acting against his parents' wishes. He chose his wife, a right that belonged to his parents, from among the Philistines - a people outside of Israel. However, God used Samson's stubbornness to encourage the Israelites, who seemed to be satisfied with the Philistine oppression.

As the story progresses, we see that Samson violated the vow he made to not contaminate himself. When he ate honey from the carcass of a lion, married a philistine and started the riddle competition, he showed his lack of maturity.

This led him to use his emotions and the incredible strength that God had given him uncontrollably.

Despite his lack of discipline, Samson never forgot the source of his strength, and God never left him.

Pre-teens need to learn that God is faithful even if we fail him. They should also know that they have the responsibility to care for their relationship with God and live in obedience and love for him.

LESSON DEVELOPMENT

Responsible

Hand out the student worksheets and write these questions on the board:

- Are you responsible?
- What privileges would you like to receive from your parents or those older than you?

Listen to the answers, and ask them to complete the acrostic suggested on their work sheet. Here we suggest some answers with which you can help those who have difficulty doing the activity.

- *Respond* with kindness when they ask me something.
- *Encourage* others
- *Say* hello to the elderly.
- *Pay* attention to the instructions of my parents and teachers.
- *Organize* my things
- *Never* be an accomplice to bad deeds.

- *Say* things that are kind
- *Intentionally* do tasks without being told
- *Be* attentive to sweeping the house
- *Let* the instructions guide me when I do homework.
- *Entertain* my little brothers when my parents are tired.

BIBLE STORY

Have students form a circle. Then, ask them: What happens when relationships between parents and children fall apart? (There will be problems if the parents fail or if the children do not fulfill their part. Every relationship, in order to be harmonious, requires work.)

In biblical times, God wanted to have a harmonious relationship with his people. But the Israelites turned their backs on him and fell into the hands of the Philistines. Then God chose to use Samson to help them see that He was superior to the pagan gods that the other people worshiped. The Nazirite vow was part of that special relationship between God and Samson. If he followed God's instructions, he would give him the strength to face the Philistines. However, something sad happened with Samson. He did not fulfill his part of the deal with God.

Read the Bible passages from the lesson and talk about what happened to this character.

The road of vengeance

Using the activity in the student worksheet, discuss the reactions that Samson had. Encourage each student to participate by answering the following questions:

1. *What was Samson's first mistake?*
   He chose a Philistine wife, ignoring his parents' advice (Judges 14:2).
2. *Why do you think Samson's parents did not want him to marry the Philistine woman?*
   The Philistines were idolaters; they worshiped Dagon. Samson's parents wanted him to choose an Israelite woman to worship the one true God (14:3).
3. *How did Samson show his great strength?*
   He killed the lion with his own hands (14:5-6).
4. *Where did Samson get the idea for the riddle?*
   He saw the bees and the honey comb in the body of the dead lion (14:8-9).
5. *What did Samson do to pay those who answered the riddle?*

He killed 30 Philistines, took their clothes and gave them to the 30 men who had answered (14:10-19).

6. *Why did Samson catch the foxes and tie burning torches to their tails?*
   He wanted revenge because his father-in-law had handed his wife over to Samson's best friend (14:20-15:5).
7. *What did the Philistines do after Samson burned their harvest?*
   They killed Samson's wife and her father. His bad actions brought about serious consequences (15:6).
8. *What did Samson do to the Philistines who wanted to catch him?*
   He killed a thousand men with the jawbone of an donkey (15:11-16).
9. *What did God do for Samson after he destroyed the Philistines?*
   Samson was tired and thirsty, so God opened a fountain of water for him to refresh himself and regain strength (15:18-20).
10. *What does this story show us about God's relationship with Samson?*
    Samson was stubborn and rebellious. He knew where his strength came from; He knew God's purpose for his life. And he was willing to use his strength against the Philistines. Despite his mistakes, God did not turn away from him and had patience.

Strengths and Weaknesses

Was it Samson's good qualities or weaknesses that got him in trouble? Discuss the results of Samson's decisions. Remind students that poor decisions lead to poor results. However, God fulfilled his promise in his relationship with Samson, giving him strength when he needed it.

Ask them to use the student worksheet to develop a list of Samson's characteristics as a person. Then, give them time to write how they imagine the story would have turned out if Samson had made good decisions (page 79).

TO FINISH

Allow time for all to respond individually to the two questions in the last activity of the student sheet, found on page 80. Then, read Philippians 4:13 together, and challenge them to make good decisions during the week.

Have a prayer time, and invite them to the next class to study the last lesson of this unit.

Lesson 22
A great loss

Biblical References: Judges 16:4-31.

Lesson objective: That the students understand that making foolish decisions always brings about bad consequences.

Memory Verse: *Trust in the Lord with all your heart and lean not on your own understanding; in all your ways submit to him, and he will make your paths straight* (Proverbs 3:5-6).

PREPARE YOURSELF TO TEACH!

It is good for preteens to know that the decisions they make will always have consequences, and some of them will affect their whole lives.

The story of Samson began full of great promises, but ended in tragedy. His bad decisions had negative effects. He forgot what the purpose of his life was, and by losing his focus, he was not careful about his actions.

Young people should reflect on the decisions they make, especially when choosing their friends.

Through the story of Samson, they will learn that when decisions are not submitted to the will of God, they always produce painful consequences. Remind them that He wants to get them away from bad decisions, and He will be faithful to help them if they seek divine wisdom.

BIBLICAL COMMENTARY

Judges 16:4-31. The story of Samson and Delilah is tragic because Samson rejected the wonderful plans that God had for his life. His foolish decisions distracted him, and he ended up blind and a slave to the Philistines. His story shows how quickly we can destroy a good relationship with God.

Samson should have left Delilah. The Bible does not say that she was a Philistine, but she had strong ties to them, and the leaders paid her to discover the secret of Samson's strength. After several false answers, he finally gave in to her persistence and revealed his secret.

As a result of such a decision, Samson lost his hair, his strength, his sight and his freedom. But the story does not end there. The Philistines did not count on the faithfulness of God. While Samson was grinding grain in the prison, his hair grew back.

In the celebration to honor the idol Dagon, the Philistines took Samson to mock him. But when he prayed for strength, God answered him. Then he knocked down the two pillars of the temple and the whole structure fell, killing him and thousands of Philistines.

Samson's story shows that making decisions without wisdom leads to destruction, but it also shows that God remains faithful, in spite of human errors.

LESSON DEVELOPMENT

Facing peer pressure

Ask the class: Have you ever felt pressured to do something that is not right? Mention some example, and allow one or two of the students to tell about a particular situation they have experienced.

Tell them that peer pressure is very strong at this stage of life. In today's lesson they will learn about a man who gave in to the pressures and suffered terrible consequences.

Show figures of artists or athletes that students know. How would they look without hair? Would it affect their voice or ability to play sports? Listen to their comments, and then introduce them to this lesson's character, who lost his hair by being pressured by a bad person.

BIBLE STORY

Depending on the number of students in your class, organize them to do the skit suggested in the student work sheets, pages 81 and 82. Another option is to choose someone to read the passage from Judges 16:4-31 and assign each person a character. Both methods require rehearsals in order to be good and capture the student's attention.

Decisions

Divide the class into small groups, pairs, or assign a question to each person, and ask them to work on the activity suggested in the work sheet, page 83. Allow a certain time for the questions to be answered.

When time's up, allow them to present their answers.

1. *When did Samson's fall begin?*

When he trusted Delilah.

2. *What could Samson have done to avoid his fall?*

Get away from Delilah. Ask for help, wisdom and strength from God.

3. *What was the result of Samson revealing his secret of Delilah?*

He broke his vows to God, he lost his strength and the Philistines captured him.

4. *What should have been some hints to Samson that he couldn't trust Delilah?*

She insisted on asking the same questions and informed the Philistines about the source of his strength.

5. *What do you think God wanted for Samson's life?*

To be obedient to his laws and use the strength he had given him.

6. *In your opinion, why did Samson's life end the way it did?*

Bad decisions = bad consequences

Write the following sentences on small cards, and give one to each of your students. They will have to take turns reading their cards. Some will read the decisions and others the respective consequences. After reading each "consequence", take time to discuss the topic. This is a good opportunity to emphasize Christian values in the lives of your students.

Decisions	Consequences
Choosing bad company.	I'll get in trouble.
Cheating on a test.	I won't learn.
Keeping something that isn't yours.	People won't trust me.
Having sex before marriage.	Unplanned pregnancy.
Insulting people.	Provokes fights.

You can add more cards, depending on the number of students.

Memory Verse

It is likely that many of your students have memorized some of the verses. We suggest that you reward them with a treat or other symbolic gift as an incentive. In this way the effort of each student is recognized.

TO FINISH

Gather your students in a circle. Pray for God to give them strength to face negative pressures from their friends, so that they always make the right decisions.

Review what they learned during these four lessons, and encourage them to attend the next class to begin to study the new unit.

CREATION

Biblical References: Genesis 1:1-28; 1:26-30; 2:15, 16-17; 3:1-24; 8:22; Job 38:1-11; Psalm 8:1-5; 8:3-9; 95:3-5; 102:25-27; Isaiah 48:12-13; Jeremiah 10:11-13; Romans 3:23; 5:8, 18-19.

Unit verse: *For you created my inmost being; you knit me together in my mother's womb. I praise you because I am fearfully and wonderfully made; your works are wonderful. I know that full well.* (Psalm 139:13-14).

The purpose of this unit:

This unit will help preteens:

- Learn about God the Creator and discover that we were created in "his image and likeness".

- Recognize the impact that sin has on our relationship with God.

- Accept the responsibility that God gave us to take care of his creation.

Unit Lessons

Lesson 23:   Our great creator

Lesson 24:   It's no accident

Lesson 25:   We are special

Lesson 26:   Sin's trap

Lesson 27:   God gave us a mission

Why do preteens need this unit?

The lessons of this unit will help your students know their origin and the reason why they were created. In these times, theories of evolution and the origin of species are increasingly popular.

The lessons will help reaffirm what students may already know: God is the Creator of the universe and the only one that has the power to breathe life into beings.

Through these teachings they will learn the differences between evolutionary theories and biblical principles about the creation of the universe.

It is important that students have the right knowledge to defend their beliefs and stand firm against the evolutionary teachings they receive at school. Help them understand that God as creator and sustainer of the universe deserves our obedience, gratitude and love.

Lesson 23
Our Great Creator

Biblical References: Genesis 1:1-28; 8:22.

Lesson objective: Students become certain that God is the one who created and sustains the universe.

Memory Verse: *For you created my inmost being; you knit me together in my mother's womb. I praise you because I am fearfully and wonderfully made; your works are wonderful. I know that full well* (Psalm 139:13-14).

PREPARE YOURSELF TO TEACH!

Most of your students have probably heard the story of creation since they were little. However, this time they will study it from another perspective. Since they know the order in which God created heaven, earth, stars, animals and man, they must now learn what it means to be part of God's magnificent creation.

In geography, biology and history books, they learn about the behavior of animals, the tumult of volcanoes and the complexity of atoms. This time they will learn to know the Creator of all these wonders.

It is our prayer that through this series of lessons, your students will learn to care for creation, honor the Creator, and understand that God created them in His image and likeness.

BIBLICAL COMMENTARY

Genesis 1:1-28; 8:22. When we read the story of creation, we realize the majesty and dominion that God has over all that exists. The Bible does not try to prove the existence of God; it only affirms that He exists (Genesis 1:1). In the midst of chaos and emptiness, God in his sovereignty turned chaos into the wonderful world that we now know and enjoy.

He created the world and everything that exists. That means that, as the Creator, everything belongs to Him.

The creation story is more than a list of what God did. It speaks to us of the very nature of God. When we read the phrase "let there be light," we realize the power and authority of God over events and nature.

The order in which he created things reveals that he is a wise God. An example of this is that He created water before fish, the sky before the birds, and he formed the earth before creating plants and animals.

The most important thing is that he is not only the Creator, but also the sustainer of everything that exists. It is by his hand that the sea does not overflow and rivers follow their natural course. However, humans often forget our place as creatures, and assume we are absolute rulers. Some even pretend to create new ways of life through science. But God created us to praise him and live in communion with him.

LESSON DEVELOPMENT

Creative Hands

For this activity you will need play-doh or handmade clay, wooden sticks and plastic tablecloths.

Before your students arrive, protect the tables with tablecloths or plastic bags. Hand out the materials. Explain to the whole class that the activity consists of using their hands and their imagination to create something found in nature. (For example: a tree, a volcano, a flower, an animal, etc.)

Then, allow each one to show their work. Explain that just as they created a figure with a piece of clay that had no form, God created the universe when there was only chaos and darkness. During this unit you will study about God, the Creator of the universe.

What a life!

Ask two volunteers to hand out the student work sheets. Then ask the class to find page 85.

Read the questions out loud for the group to answer, and write down the answers on the board. Then, talk about the importance of trees in nature.

Explain that trees produce oxygen. In addition, their wood is used to make houses, furniture, pencils, paper, etc.

Follow the clues

Have students turn to page 86. Ask them to carefully observe the picture and identify the child's favorite activities and list them on the board.

Then, ask them: In what ways can someone tell you what kind of person this boy is?

Based on the list, determine some of the characteristics of this child's personality. For example, the illustration shows that he is interested in music. This activity requires patience to learn to play a new instrument and determination to practice continuously. He also seems to like sports. This activity requires physical dexterity and discipline. Etc.

To conclude the activity, tell them: Through this child's favorite activities, we know part of his personality. Today we will study creation and learn what it tells us about God's personality.

BIBLE STORY

Choose one of the following methods to teach the story: Tell the story of creation in your own words, let your students read it from the Bible or use visual materials to explain the narrative.

Remember that you should always have the Bible in a visible place, so your students will know that it is a story mentioned in the Word of God.

It is likely that many of your students know the details of the story. Therefore, we suggest you allow them to actively participate in the lesson as you tell it.

ACTIVITIES

Only God could make...

Hand out sheets of paper and colored pencils. Ask your students to write the title "Only God could make ..." Then, have them draw a picture of what only he can make.

Each student must go to the front, and showing their finished work, say, "Only God could make ... (volcanoes, rivers, snow, etc.)".

Place all the works in a visible place to form a mural of creation, which will be added to with each lesson of the unit.

Find the answers to your questions

Divide the class in pairs. Then, ask them to look up the verses suggested in the concordance on page 87 of their work sheets.

Then, have them write the biblical references that corresponds to each phrase in the lower part.

1. God created the world (Mark 13:19).
2. Everything that God created is good (1 Timothy 4:4)
3. God created man in his own image (Genesis 1:27)
4. If anyone is in Christ, the new creation has come (2 Corinthians 5:17).
5. You must remember your Creator while you are young (Ecclesiastes 12:1).
6. Since the creation of the world, the invisible qualities of God have been clearly seen (Romans 1:20).

What does creation show you about...?

Once again, divide the class into pairs to answer the questions on page 88 of the work sheet. Tell them to talk about what they learned about God in the creation story.

Then, each couple will must share their answers with the others.

TO FINISH

Ask your students to look up Psalm 139:13-14 in their Bibles and read it out loud. Explain that this is this unit's memory verse, and tell them: God made the world and created humans. However, sometimes we forget how wonderful our bodies are, having been made by him. This verse will remind us of the importance of knowing that we were created by God to praise Him.

Review the memory verse a couple of times. Then, give God thanks for his wonderful creation and for allowing us to know him through it.

Lesson 24

It's no accident!

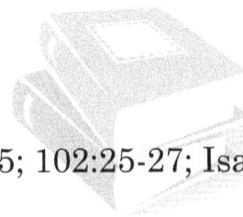

Biblical References: Genesis 1:1, 27; Job 38:1-11; Psalm 95:3-5; 102:25-27; Isaiah 48:12-13; Jeremiah 10:11-13.

Lesson objective: That the students understand that the origin of life and the universe come from God, the creator.

Memory Verse: *For you created my inmost being; you knit me together in my mother's womb. I praise you because I am fearfully and wonderfully made; your works are wonderful. I know that full well* (Psalm 139:13-14).

PREPARE YOURSELF TO TEACH!

Science and faith are not two words that are commonly related. On the contrary, society is responsible for separating them. Many secular teachers use the theory of species and evolution to refute their students' religious beliefs.

Pre-teens need to remain steadfast in the truth that God is the Creator, and understand that science is effective for learning about the physical world. That is, science existed after creation, but explaining the origin of creation belongs to the field of faith.

At this stage of their school life, students will begin to study the origin of species and other theories of evolution. This argues that everything was created by a cosmic explosion, or that living beings were bacteria that mutated, becoming complex organisms. That is why it is important that students learn what the Word says on this subject, and that they know that God is the only creator, owner and Lord of all that exists.

Ask for the guidance of the Holy Spirit so that, through this lesson, pre-teens will know how to defend their beliefs and stand firm in the truth of the Word of God.

BIBLICAL COMMENTARY

Genesis 1:1. In the Bible, we find evidence of God as the creator. The first verse of the Bible says, "In the beginning God created." That means that God existed before everything.

Job 38:1-11. In this conversation, God talks with Job about the mysteries and secrets of creation. God's description of the world is so complex and wonderful that people cannot fully understand it. God is the architect of the world and only he deserves our worship and service.

Psalm 95:3-5; 102:25-27. These verses describe God as the creator. Human beings were created to worship and praise God for his rule over the world.

Isaiah 48:12-13. Isaiah recognizes God as the creator, the only true God. He is trustworthy, and people must believe in him as being sovereign.

Jeremiah 10:11-13. Jeremiah gives a message to the Hebrews in exile. His warning includes judgment against worshipping idols, but also affirms that God is the only creator of the world..

LESSON DEVELOPMENT

Identify the objects

Before class, put 15 different objects in a bag (for example: a spoon, a coin, a ribbon, cotton, a rattle, etc.). Make a list of the objects, and choose four participants for this activity.

Ask the four people to leave the room. Then, call them back in one at a time.

Ask the first one to touch the objects inside the bag and guess what they are. Then let him write his answers down.

The second student should shake the bag, guess the content through the sounds and make his own list.

Call the third person in and have him look inside the bag for three seconds and write down what objects he saw.

Hide the bag

Then, ask the fourth student to come forward and say: A while ago I put several objects in this bag and made a list of the contents. Now read this list and tell me which objects you think I put in the bag.

Compare the lists they made and show the objects that were in the bag to the rest of the group. Emphasize that the four participants were describing the same objects, but each one did it in a different way.

Explain that people also use different means to understand the origin of our world. Some use science to understand the physical point of view and others resort to biblical principles. In today's story, we will learn what the differences between these two points of view are.

Same or different?

Hand out the student work sheets, and ask the young people to go to page 89. There they should read the biblical and scientific statements.

Divide them into small groups so that they can discuss about why they should or should not believe such claims. Each group will appoint a secretary who will write down the conclusions and then report their answers to the class.

BIBLE STORY

Tell your students: The Bible tells us about creation in the book of Genesis. However, other biblical passages also bear witness that God was the creator. Today we will explore what the Bible tells us about God and his creation.

Divide them into three groups, and make sure that each group has a Bible. After assigning the questions from page 90 to the groups, ask them to look up the passages and find the answers. When everyone has finished, ask them to comment on the conclusions they reached.

ACTIVITIES

Creation mural

For this activity you will need cardboard, glue, scissors, colored markers, pencils and objects from nature that your students have collected (leaves, stones, flowers, twigs, etc.).

Instruct them to use the materials to create a mural about creation. As they work, encourage them to praise God for his wonderful creation.

When they are finished, place the mural on the classroom door for parents and family to see.

Science or religion?

Look at the illustration on page 91, and identify which phrases correspond to the scientific point of view.

Explain to your students that many people try to disprove biblical truth with scientific theories. But God is clear in affirming that he created heaven, earth and everything that exists.

Tell them that when confronted with these ideologies, they should remain firm in the knowledge of God as the sole Lord and creator of the universe.

Can you explain...?

Ask preteens if they know how televisions receive signals, and transform them into images and sounds. Listen to their answers and ask: So, why do you keep watching the programs that are broadcast?

Follow the suggested examples in the student worksheet and give them time to write the answers. Conclude by explaining that there are some aspects of creation that we may never fully understand. Only God knows everything, because he is the creator of the universe. But that does not prevent us from trusting in his power and sovereignty.

TO FINISH

Pray and give thanks to God for his creation and the blessing of being a part of it. Sing some worship songs and review the memory verse before dismissal.

We Are Special

Biblical References: Genesis 1:26-30; Psalm 8:1-5.

Lesson Objective: That the preteens learn the honor, privilege, and responsibility that we have since we are created in God's image and likeness.

Memory Verse: *For you created my inmost being; you knit me together in my mother's womb. I praise you because I am fearfully and wonderfully made; your works are wonderful. I know that full well* (Psalm 139:13-14).

PREPARE YOURSELF TO TEACH!

Preadolescents go through a stage in their life in which self-esteem problems are common. In some cases, their self-esteem is so high that they become arrogant, while in others, their lack of self-love makes them feel insecure and inferior.

When your students understand that God created them in his image and likeness, they will realize that value and respect are an important part of God's wonderful creation.

Stereotypes of beauty, high social demands, emotional and physical abuse - even abandonment, can make your students feel that they are inferior and that they are not important in this world. Therefore, take advantage of this lesson to help them understand that they are special and important in the eyes of God, the king of the universe.

BIBLICAL COMMENTARY

Genesis 1:26-30. God created human beings in his image. That does not mean that we are physically equal to him; instead, it means that we are similar in intelligence, in emotions, will, responsibility and spirit.

We were also given the capability to understand and to have free will. In addition, we can learn, love and obey our Creator.

Before the fall, Adam and Eve could rule the earth without the fear of being wrong. Their desires were pure and they had full freedom; they even communicated with God face to face.

It is important to understand that God values people, placing them above the rest of creation. However, being made in the "image of God" entails a responsibilities, in addition to honor and privilege.

Psalm 8:1-5. This psalm helps us to understand the value that God gives to people. Even though we are insignificant when compared to the wonderful universe, God gives us a place of honor in creation. It reminds us that he made us worthy before his eyes; that is why we must give him honor and glory forever.

LESSON DEVELOPMENT

Paper men

For this activity you will need newspapers or recycled paper, scissors and colored markers. Move the tables and chairs, leaving a space for your students to work on the floor. Ask them to use the newspaper to make an image of themselves (for example, they can lie down on the newspaper and ask a partner to draw their silhouette and then decorate it with colored markers).

Then ask them: Was it easy or hard to create an image of yourself with the materials you had? Does the figure you made reflect anything of your personality? After listening to their answers, tell them that in today's Bible story, they will talk about what it means that God made us according to his image and likeness.

No to rejection!

Ask your students to talk about the questions on page 93 of their worksheets, and then write the answers in the blanks.

Emphasize the fact that we all have days when we are sad and feel discouraged and are even unhappy with ourselves. There are individuals who have low self-esteem, that is, they think that they have no or little value as people. In today's lesson, we will learn what it means that God made us in His image and why that makes us valuable.

BIBLE STORY

Let your students sit in a circle, and tell them: In the previous lessons we learned about God and his creation. We also saw that his love, beauty and wisdom are revealed in the majesty of his creation.

After creating

Ask your students to look up Genesis 1:26-30 and read it.

Then, ask them: Why did God make mankind different than the rest of creation? What does God think about the people he created? Why are humans important to God?

Read the study passages, and write the answers on the board. When talking about the importance that human have in creation, emphasize that regardless of the flaws we may have, God looks at us with love and considers us his special creation.

ACTIVITIES

What is the image of God?

Allow students to read the paragraph on page 94 of their worksheets. Explain that the divine image in a person is not physical. God is a Spirit - that is, he does not possess form or a body like ours. However, he gave us his same spiritual nature. This spiritual quality is what makes us unique, and distinguishes us from other created beings. In addition, it allows us to have communication and communion with God.

Give them time to read the three questions at the bottom of the page. Instruct them to look up the answers in the paragraph and underline them.

My qualities

For this activity you will need sheets of paper, pencils and tape.

Through this activity, pre-teens should recognize the qualities of others and, at the same time, understand what others think about them. Tape a sheet of paper onto the back of each student, and give everyone a pencil.

Everyone should write on their colleagues' paper some of their good qualities (for example: friendly, kind, helpful, cheerful, etc.).

Emphasize that comments should be positive. They must be very careful not to write anything that is hurtful.

When everyone has written something about others, write some of God's qualities on the board: merciful, loving, fair, compassionate, patient, etc.

Compare the lists from people's backs with the characteristics written on the board. Then, encourage them to try to live each day in the image and likeness of God. Congratulate those who demonstrated Christian behavior, and encourage those who are trying to do so. Remember that for this type of lesson the example you give as their teacher is very important.

TO FINISH

Write the memory verse on the board (Psalm 139:13-14), and read it together. Then repeat it as you erase it word by word, until the board is empty and students can say the text by heart.

Ask two volunteers to lead the prayer time. Let the first student intercede for special requests and for the sick, and the second give thanks to God for having created us in His image and likeness.

Say goodbye by singing a song of praise to God, and remember to invite them to class next week to continue studying about creation.

Lesson 26
Sin's trap

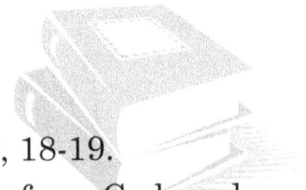

Biblical References: Genesis 2:16-17; 3:1-24; Romans 3:23; 5:8, 18-19.

Lesson objective: That the preteens learn that sin separates us from God, and decide to strengthen their relationship with the Lord.

Memory Verse: *For you created my inmost being; you knit me together in my mother's womb. I praise you because I am fearfully and wonderfully made; your works are wonderful. I know that full well* (Psalm 139:13-14).

PREPARE YOURSELF TO TEACH!

It is important that your students understand that we all face different temptations. Now that young people begin to make more important decisions, they must be alert not to fall into the trap of sin.

Explain that sometimes temptation is presented in a very subtle way, making us believe that there is nothing wrong with it. However, the results are tragic and always affect the lives of other people.

Since sin entered the world, human beings have been inclined towards disobedience and evil. Only through the grace of God can we have our relationship with him restored and find forgiveness for our sins.

BIBLICAL COMMENTARY

Genesis 2:16-17; 3:1-24. If God's creation is so wonderful, where did evil come from? These passages answer the question. The verses clearly show us that God is not responsible for the wickedness of the world. He gave Adam and Eve wonderful gifts. The Garden of Eden was an idyllic place to live, and He gave them the freedom to make their own decisions. In addition, they could eat all the fruits of the garden, except one.

But, the snake knew how to tempt them. Appealing to human appetites, he offered the fruit to Eve, and aroused in her the desire for wisdom and power.

At first, the idea did not seem to please Eve, but as the serpent continued to speak to her, her heart became convinced of his lies and deliberately disobeyed God. From that moment, the change in the history of humanity was drastic. Sin separated man from God. Fear, shame, anxiety and worry were then present in Adam and Eve's lives.

The weakness of Adam and Eve has caused thousands of years of pain, tears, wars and suffering.

The Bible is clear when it says that God does not tolerate sin, and that the wages of sin is death.

However, God does not leave his people without hope. Through Jesus, sinners can receive forgiveness and have their relationship with God restored.

LESSON DEVELOPMENT

What's the price?

Have your students sit in a circle, and ask them if they think there are certain things that are better not to know or learn. Write down their answers on the board. Then explain that people who have tried drugs, tobacco, liquor, have seen pornography, etc. hurt themselves and others in this process.

It is not good that we try to experiment with what is bad, because the price can be too high, including problems and pain. Today's Bible story is a good example of this.

Temptation

Write each of the following questions on small pieces of paper:

- What does "temptation" mean?
- How can preteens push others to fall into temptation?

- What is the worst temptation for them?
- What kind of people face temptation?

Fold the pieces of paper, and insert each one into a balloon. Inflate the balloons and hang them around the room.

Allow students to pop a balloon and answer the question that they get. After listening to the answers, tell them that today's story tells us about a couple who faced temptation.

BIBLE STORY

Ask your group to pay special attention to the techniques the tempter used to convince Adam and Eve to disobey God.

Assign two students to read Genesis 2:16-17 and Genesis 3:1-19 aloud, while others follow along. Finally, read Genesis 3:22-24 together.

- What gifts did God give to Adam and Eve?
- What techniques did the snake use to tempt them?
- What was it that convinced them to disobey?
- What were the results of Adam and Eve's disobedience?

ACTIVITIES

Why was it so wrong to eat the fruit?

Ask the young people: Why do you think God got so angry with Adam and Eve? Was it so bad to eat a fruit? Allow them to respond. Then, emphasize that eating the fruit was not the sinful part, rather it was disobeying God. Sin destroyed their communion with God.

Then ask: What do we learn about God in this story?

God is just and does not tolerate sin; that is why He had to expel Adam and Eve from the garden.

However, God is not a dictator. He gives us the right to choose freely. Adam and Eve chose to listen to the tempter, distrust God and fall into the trap of sin.

Beware of the trap!

Ask your students to go to page 96, and there they will find their way through the traps of temptation. Have them read the Bible verses to see what temptations Adam and Eve faced.

Talk about the sins that Adam and Eve committed when they fell into the trap of temptation (ex. disobedience, rebellion, distrust of God, etc.).

Divide the class into pairs or small groups. Give them time to discuss the possible answers to this question. Then they can write their conclusions in the space indicated on page 97.

How does God help us when we're tempted?

Many people have an incorrect concept of the way God intervenes when Christians face temptations. Through this activity, teach your students the biblical principles about it.

Ask them to read the sentences on page 97 of their book. Instruct them to write an "A" if they agree, and a "D" if they disagree with what is written there.

Review the answers, and explain how God helps us resist temptation. However, each one of us is responsible for choosing whether to obey God's voice or not.

Finally, direct your students' attention to page 98 and explain the steps of the salvation plan. Ask your students if anyone wishes to restore their relationship with God, and if so, lead them in prayer.

Encourage those who accepted Christ. During the week, set aside time to visit them and confirm their decision.

TO FINISH

Sing songs of praise, and repeat the memory verse before saying goodbye.

Ask the students to investigate an animal that is in danger of extinction during the week so that they can then tell the group about it in the next class.

Lesson 27
God gave us a mission

Biblical References: Genesis 1:26-30; 2:15; Psalm 8:3-9.

Lesson Objective: That the preteens learn that it is their responsibility to take care of God's creation.

Memory Verse: *For you created my inmost being; you knit me together in my mother's womb. I praise you because I am fearfully and wonderfully made; your works are wonderful. I know that full well* (Psalm 139:13-14).

PREPARE YOURSELF TO TEACH!

It is common for the media, schools and other educational centers to care for the environment and ecology. In many places, campaigns are organized to conserve water, recycle garbage, and protect endangered species or green areas that have not yet been deforested.

However, taking care of creation has been the responsibility of the people of God long before environmental movements emerged. This lesson will help students understand that taking care of the world that God created is the task of Christians because we are his stewards.

God created the world, and gave us the responsibility to care for and protect it. We are responsible to him for the way we use his creation. That is why it is important to study what the Bible tells us about this subject.

This lesson will help your students know the responsibility they have as stewards of the Lord.

BIBLICAL COMMENTARY

Genesis 1:26-30; 2:15; Psalm 8:3-9. God gave the first human beings the responsibility to care for and protect the Garden of Eden. He gave special value to heaven, earth, stars and everything that existed. He also allowed humans to enjoy and benefit from creation; but this privilege implied a responsibility: to care for and preserve it.

After the first sin, this task became more complex. Thistles and thorns made it harder to sow and harvest, and people misused natural resources and animals.

Nowadays, we are also God's stewards. Therefore, we have the obligation to protect, care for and preserve the world that he created with so much love for us.

LESSON DEVELOPMENT

Take care of the environment!

During the week, look in magazines or newspapers for advertisements of environmental groups, or illustrations on how to take care of the environment (for example, phrases such as: "throw the garbage in the dump", "take care of the trees", etc.).

Show the students what you found, and ask what they mean. Allow them to suggest other ways to care for nature and then write them on the board.

Explain that long before there was environmental care and ecology, God assigned his people the task of caring for and preserving his creation. In today's Bible story, we will learn more about this subject.

Report from outer space

Hand out the student worksheets and ask them to turn to page 99. Tell them to imagine that they are explorers from another planet. Their mission is to observe how the inhabitants of the earth take care of their world and in what condition it is.

Ask them to form pairs or small groups to prepare their report, following along with the questions suggested in the worksheet. Then, they must give their conclusions to the whole class. Tell them that in today's story they will learn about a special mission that God gave to his people.

BIBLE STORY

To teach this lesson's biblical truth, we suggest you use the activity on the page 100 of the student worksheet.

They can work together or in small groups. Ask a volunteer to read Genesis 1:26-30; 2:15; and let another read Psalms 8:3-9. Then, give them time to read the comment on page 100 and answer the questions below.

While they are working, be attentive to help them if there are questions, if the members of a group do not agree, or if it is necessary to complement their answers with more information. The goal is to clearly understand that God is the creator of everything, and that we are the stewards of His creation.

ACTIVITIES

In danger of being extinct!

Ask your students if they remembered to investigate about an animal that is in danger of extinction. Ask that some come forward to give a brief explanation about the animal they studied. Tell them that "extinct" means that all if that particular animal have died and no longer exist.

Have them find page 101, and ask them to draw some extinct animals (for example: the dodo bird, the sea cow, the mammoth, the imperial woodpecker, the saber-toothed tiger, etc.). Try to get pictures with illustrations of these animals so that your students can copy them. If it is not possible, ask them to only write the names of these animals.

Next, draw some animals that are in danger of extinction (for example: the giant panda, the Siberian tiger, the imperial eagle, the gray or grizzly bear, the Nile crocodile, the giant otter, the gorilla, etc.).

Talk about what they can do to help protect these species and care for God's creation.

Newspaper

Divide the class into pairs again. Ask them to turn the page and talk about some ways to care for creation.

Also, ask that each group write an article about a way to protect the environment. In the end, they can show their work to the whole class.

My commitment

Before the class begins, make several "commitment letters", guided by the following model:

On this date, _____ (date), I will commit myself to _____ (conserve water, recycle take out the trash, etc.) to fulfill my responsibility as God's steward and take care of the creation he made.

_____(Signature)

Leave the underlined spaces blank for your students to fill out and sign their letter. Allow them to take the letter home as a reminder. Emphasize that they must fulfill their commitment.

TO FINISH

Give thanks to God for the things you all have studied in this unit, and if there is still time, make a general review.

Remind them that God is the creator of everything that exists. That is why He deserves our obedience, loyalty and love. Also encourage them to take care of nature and protect the environment.

If you wish, reward those who memorized the unit verse, and tell them that next week they will begin to study the unit entitled "Let's live like Christ."

Let's live like Christ

Biblical References: Mark 9:38-40; 10:35-43; Luke 9:51-56; John 19:25-27; 20:1-9; Romans 12:2; 1 John 1:7; 1:5-10; 2:1-11, 15-17; 3:1-24; 4:7-19; 2:18-27; 4:1-6; 2 John 9.

Unit verse: *But if we walk in the light, as he is in the light, we have fellowship with one another, and the blood of Jesus, his Son, purifies us from all sin* (1 John 1:7).

The purpose of this unit

This unit will help preteens to:

- Understand that love is a distinctive characteristic of Christians.
- Understand the importance of love and obedience to God.
- Learn to be more loving with God and with their neighbor.
- Understand and discern that there are false religious ideas which should be evaluated in the light of the Bible.

Unit Lessons

Lesson 28: A different life

Lesson 29: Let's live like Jesus

Lesson 30: Love is the key

Lesson 31: What do we believe?

Why do preteens need this unit?

It is common for minors to carefully observe the behavior of older people, trying to find models of behavior that they can imitate. In particular, the influence of the media can corrupt children and adults because it presents them with lifestyles different than the purity and holiness that the Bible teaches. It is during this stage of transition that they begin to think independently and seek answers everywhere. In reality, what they seek is to define their own identity, which includes the spiritual aspect, although many times they do the opposite.

Through the writings of John, preteens will learn more about some aspects of the Christian life. John teaches us the importance of a loving obedience to God, and that love is not only a feeling, but also action. They will realize that God shows them his love, and therefore, they will want to show that love to their neighbor.

These lessons will help your students mature in their spiritual growth and understand the true meaning of love. Remember that just as Christians in the early church faced false teachings and philosophies, students today hear teachings that are contrary to the Word of God. Through these lessons, explain that we should ask God for discernment to get away from the false doctrines that threaten our faith.

A different life

Biblical References: Mark 9:38-40; 10:35-43; Luke 9:51-56; John 19:25-27; 20:1-9; Romans 12:2; 1 John 1:7.

Lesson Objective: Preteens learn that God has the power to transform lives.

Memory Verse: *But if we walk in the light, as he is in the light, we have fellowship with one another, and the blood of Jesus, his Son, purifies us from all sin* (1 John 1:7).

PREPARE YOURSELF TO TEACH!

During this stage of their development, pre-adolescents face a series of significant changes in their lives. They leave childhood behind and begin adolescence. Their body and their emotions change. Their perspective on the world and the way they relate to others is also different.

But the most important thing is that these changes have an impact on their spiritual life. It is during this period that they begin to question their faith. They no longer believe only because the teacher says so; now they want to check out for themselves the legitimacy of the Bible, looking for specific examples of a genuine Christian life.

Therefore, it is very important that as a teacher you are not only a "source of knowledge", but that you also encourage your students to reflect and analyze things in light of the Word of God. What your students learn in class will be significant only if they actively participate- by reading the Word, talking and praying- and, above all, by applying the biblical principles in their daily lives.

BIBLICAL COMMENTARY

In this lesson several biblical passages were put together to make a small biography of the apostle John.

He was one of the privileged men who walked near Jesus and met him in person. Jesus asked him to be his disciple, and he formed part of his inner circle. Commentators know him as "the beloved disciple." He witnessed the resurrection of Jairus' daughter; He was close to Jesus in the Garden of Gethsemane; He was also present at the crucifixion and received the task of taking care of Mary, the mother of his teacher. In addition, he was the first disciple who understood the meaning of the empty tomb.

After Jesus' ascension, John became the leader of the church, and wrote letters to encourage and comfort the new Christians. Three of those letters are in the New Testament.

Later, John was exiled to a rocky island, called Patmos. There he lived as a prisoner, doing jobs in the field. It was in that place that he received an amazing vision of Jesus Christ as the eternal Lord of all time.

The Revelation was the message of strength and security that God gave to his people in 90 AD, when he suffered intense persecution for refusing to worship the Roman gods. Not only that, but it is a letter of encouragement for us as well. However, John was not perfect when Jesus chose him as his disciple. He was known as one of "the sons of thunder," and his character needed to be molded. Through this lesson the Lord reminds us that he can use imperfect people and transform them by his grace.

Lesson development

What changes?

Gather your students in a circle. Ask them if they know any person who lived in sin before, but after knowing Christ began to live a different lifestyle. Listen to the answers, and use them as a basis to introduce this unit's topic. Then, encourage them to discover in the Bible the biography of a man whose life was transformed by Jesus Christ.

Who is it?

Hand out paper and pencils so your students can write a short biography of a familiar character. Ask some volunteers to read what they wrote so that their classmates guess who the description refers to.

Point out that today's lesson is about a man who wrote about the life of Jesus.

BIBLE STORY

Considering that preadolescents have some difficulty participating, we suggest this activity so that they not only receive knowledge, but they are the ones who discover the biblical truths by reading their Bible.

Divide the group in two investigative teams. The first group must read the passages about the life of John as a "son of thunder" (Mark 9:38-40; 10:35-43; Luke 9:51-56) and write down the results on one side of the board; the second group should read the passages of John's life as a disciple of Jesus (John 19:25-27; 20:1-9) and write their notes on the other side. Then, both teams should compare the results and write them in the student worksheet. Emphasize the change that John made when he met Christ.

ACTIVITIES

Evidence of change

Have then turn to page 104 in the student's worksheets to read and analyze the biblical passages. Then, give them time to write down the changes in John's life.

Talk about how John's writings show the change in his life. Then, reflect on the evidence of change that must be present in the lives of those who know Christ. Then let them write examples of young people who have a problem similar to the one John had.

Special report

Direct your students' attention to page 106 of the student worksheet, and divide the group into pairs.

Assign each pair one of the five cards that describe John and have them study it for a few minutes.

Explain that they should pretend to be television anchors for a program called "Awesome people and events." Therefore, they should prepare a special report for a documentary about the life of John, using the information on the cards as the basis of information.

Have some props that they can use to stage this activity, for example: costumes, a microphone, etc.

Love in action

We suggest that during this month your students develop a project outside of class, in which they get involved to show love towards their neighbors (for example: they could collect clothes and food to take them to a community in need; help the elderly; feed children from the street; visit the sick, etc.).

Bookmarks for your Bible

Provide scissors for your students to make the suggested bookmark on page 106 of the activity book, and take it home. We recommend you stick the bookmark on cardboard or paperboard to make it more sturdy. This will help them memorize the books of the New Testament.

TO FINISH

Gather your students to pray and intercede for their needs. Remind them that in the same way that God changed John's life, he can also change theirs.

If the Holy Spirit moves you, invite them to accept Christ as their personal Lord and savior; Lead them in the prayer of salvation. Remember to disciple the students who accepted Christ during the week, and encourage them to attend next week. Say goodbye by repeating the memory verse.

Let's live like Jesus

Biblical References: 1 John 1:5-10; 2:1-11, 15-17

Lesson objective: That the preteens learn that obeying God will help them grow in their spiritual life.

Memory Verse: *But if we walk in the light, as he is in the light, we have fellowship with one another, and the blood of Jesus, his Son, purifies us from all sin* (1 John 1:7).

PREPARE YOURSELF TO TEACH!

No matter which country we live in, it is a fact that all societies are going through a serious crisis of values. We have reached the point of legalizing sin and justifying the violation of God's law in favor of scientific advance or modernism.

Therefore, it is not surprising that we barely have a vague concept about what it means to live like Jesus. This does not imply that we do not know what it is to live in righteousness, but that we do not have the appropriate models of behavior. Television, radio, movies and fashion have been responsible for distorting biblical values.

Even your students are likely to live in homes where violence dominates or where sin is acceptable. So, how can they know if their way of living is correct?

It is important that, even in such an inconsistent society, they learn that Jesus is the perfect model. Through this lesson, students will learn that it is possible to live as Jesus did. They just need to be willing to acknowledge their sins and to take hold of God's hand to obey Him out of love.

BIBLICAL COMMENTARY

The Bible tells us that God is light, and when He illuminates us, He reveals our true nature. When a person walks in darkness, he needs courage to take a step of faith and approach the intense and penetrating light that exposes all his imperfections and spiritual faults. Jesus Christ gave his life to cleanse us and allow us to walk in the light.

This means living as Christ did, away from sin, and cultivating a close relationship with God that allows us to bear abundant fruit.

Living like Jesus also means being honest with God, with ourselves and with others, as well as obeying His Word.

Being obedient is a test of our love for God. Slaves obey because they have no choice. Employees obey because they need their job. However, Christians obey the Father because they wish to do so, and it is a fundamental part of the relationship of love between them.

John gives us two keys that help us determine if we are living like Jesus: when we confess our sins and restore our relationship with the Father, and when we demonstrate our love for our neighbor.

LESSON DEVELOPMENT

Where do you walk?

Start the class by asking two volunteers to bind their eyes with a handkerchief and try to walk around the room. Remove all objects that may hurt them.

Ask them to remove the bandage and explain how they felt when walking while being blind. Tell the group that the same thing happens in our lives if we do not have Christ; we walk in the darkness of sin, without a guide or knowing the right direction. However, there is hope if we change course and ask Christ to direct our path.

BIBLE STORY

Before class, make a photocopy of the letter that appears after this explanation and put it in an envelope. Give it to a member of your church, and ask him to present it to your students at the front of the class.

Ask the preteens to sit in a circle. Tell them: In the previous lesson, we studied the life of the apostle John, and we learned that

God transforms the lives of those who choose to follow him. Now listen carefully to the following letter and at the end, we will talk about the meaning of its content.

Dear brothers:

I learned that some Christians have stopped attending church, and began to gather together to form a new congregation. Normally this should be joyous news; however, they are not teaching the Word of God, and they have confused many people. Watch out for false teachers and keep the truth of the gospel that you heard from me.

Keep loving God and your neighbors, and remember that God is light. When you allow God to live in you, the darkness moves away, because he is the light that fills all areas of your life. On the contrary, if you continue in sin, the light will go away from you. Meditate on this.

For example, when your room is dark and you cannot see the furniture, is the furniture still there? Of course! However, only light helps us see clearly.

That is why we say that Christ is the light, because only he can show us the clear truth of his Word. When we obey those truths, we are "walking in the light." Obeying the Word of God is a sign that we love Christ.

Jesus promised that he would be our light and that he would walk beside us. He cannot walk where there is darkness or sin, because he is light. So if someone says he belongs to Christ, but he continues to sin, he is lying.

Now, how can they know if they are walking in the light? If you have confessed your sins before God, be assured that you were forgiven. In this way you can feel the love of God for you and express it to others.

Follow Christ and remain faithful to his Word. I have a lot to tell you, but I prefer not to do it by letter. I hope to visit you soon to speak to you in person. I will be very happy. Greetings to all of you

Your brother, John.

ACTIVITIES

Walking in the light

Ask the pre-teens to open their student worksheets to page 107, and look for the suggested biblical passages. Encourage a discussion about the meaning of the passages and what they mean for their lives. Give time for your students to write their conclusions.

What does the Bible say?

Instruct them to turn the page, and work in pairs or small groups. Then read 1 John 1:5-10 and 2:1-11, and connect each Bible verse with its correct meaning.

Stay attentive to them, and help them when they struggle to connect both columns.

Why should we walk in the light?

Allow time for students to look at the drawings on page 109 of their books and fill in the blanks with the correct answer.

As they work, talk about the importance of living like Jesus and reflecting the light of Christ to others.

Next, turn the page and read 1 John 2:6 aloud. Write on the board the three questions at the bottom of the page, and let them all answer them together. Write the conclusions on the board, and give them time to copy them on their worksheet.

TO FINISH

Encourage your students to reflect on the light and the character of Christ during the week. Suggest some ways in which they can do it (for example: help with chores, obey parents and teachers, be kind to peers, preach the gospel, pray for the sick, etc.).

Then, ask two students to intercede for prayer requests, and conclude with a final prayer, asking the Lord to help the young people grow in their spiritual life.

Repeat the memory verse a couple of times and invite them to next week's class to study the last lesson of this unit.

Lesson 30

Love is the key

Biblical References: 1 John 3:1-24; 4:7-19.

Lesson Objective: Preteens learn that we cannot love others without the love of God.

Memory Verse: *But if we walk in the light, as he is in the light, we have fellowship with one another, and the blood of Jesus, his Son, purifies us from all sin* (1 John 1:7).

PREPARE YOURSELF TO TEACH!

In our vocabulary, one of the most commonly used words is "love". However, the meaning that society gives to this word is very different from the one found in the Bible.

It is likely that your students have a misconception about love. For this reason, it is very important that through these lessons they understand what God tells us about it. They must know that God is the source of love and that only in him do we find perfect love.

Remember that as a teacher, your life should be a living example of God's love reflected to your students. The way you treat, care for, and address them will teach them how Christians should love one another.

At this stage in which preadolescents seek to find their identity within their groups, and feel like they belong to it, they tend to select the people with whom they wish to connect, and sometimes exclude others. For that reason, they must learn that God loves all people, without discriminating against anyone.

Take into account that all your students come from very different family and social backgrounds. Maybe some have not received love in their family, and for that reason they find it difficult to understand this concept. Help them understand that God's love is perfect and unconditional, and available to all who wish to receive it.

BIBLICAL COMMENTARY

1 John 3:1-24; 4:7-19. In these passages of the Bible, John writes about remaining steadfast in the knowledge of Christ and the importance of love. This letter was addressed to a congregation that was just beginning to grow in their Christian faith. Some false teachers had placed doubt in the new members about their trust in God's love, so they had began to question their relationship of love with the Lord.

John begins by talking about the real foundation of love: God is love. Love is not just one of the qualities or attributes of God, but it is part of his nature. This explains why he sent Jesus, his only Son, to pay the price for our salvation.

When we convert to Christianity, we experience his love, and this love motivates us to love our neighbor. Love is the evidence of our life in Christ. True love translates into action, not just feelings and words.

John tells us that the person who has been born of God does not continue to sin, and reminds us that Christians must turn away from evil.

LESSON DEVELOPMENT

John is considered the apostle of love, since in all his writings he manifests a genuine love for God and his brothers. As we study John's first letter, we will learn what God tells us about love.

To begin, write the following question on the board: How many kinds of love exist and what are they? Hand out the student's worksheets and allow the preteens to write on their hearts the different types of love

83

that exist. Then, explain the three most important kinds of love (eros, phyla and agape), and tell them that in this lesson they will study the divine concept of love.

Searching for love

Divide the group into teams, and ask them to complete the activity on page 112 of the student sheet. They should look up the concordance passages in their Bible and, based on these, answer the five questions.

Make sure each team has at least one Bible, and if new students attend, include one on each team to help them integrate into the class. Be attentive to solve any doubt or question that may arise.

BIBLE STORY

To present today's Bible story, we suggest that you read the study passages in advance and write your conclusions on a card. This will help you easily remember the most important points.

You will also need a keyring with seven keys that you no longer use. Prepare seven small stickers (which can be stuck on the keys), and number them from 1 to 7. Then, write on each one the corresponding phrase according to the number: 1. God is love. 2. When we are Christians we feel his love. 3. God's love helps us love others. 4. True love is action, not just words. 5. God loved us first. 6. God showed us his love by sending Jesus. 7. God wants us to grow in knowledge and love.

Glue a card on the key ring that says "Love is the key". Hand out the keys, and ask everyone to read their sentences out loud. While narrating the Bible story, use the keys to represent each of the concepts John points out in these passages. Each time you use a key, ask the student to put it on the key ring.

Then hang the key ring at the entrance to the classroom, and use it as a reminder of what you learned in this lesson.

ACTIVITIES

Demonstrations of love

Ask the class to find page 113 in their worksheets and ask them what they think when they are looking at the illustration.

Listen to their answers and, based on them, explain the importance of the sacrifice of Christ as a demonstration of God's love. Give them time to complete the blanks in the verse, and repeat it together a couple of times.

Then, reflect on what they can do to show God that they love Him. Ask them to write their answers at the bottom of the page. If you have time, have them share their answers with the rest of the group.

Love is...

Ask your students to come together in pairs to work on the activity on page 114. They should complete the sentences, filling in the blanks with examples of the way in which love manifests itself in a specific situation. For example: Love is: forgiving someone when they hurt you.

When they finish, exchange the books with each other and read the answers out loud.

Love in action

If they decided to organize a social aid project or were involved in a ministry, today is the day to evaluate the work they have done and the results.

Let everyone express how they felt while speaking to their neighbor about the love of God.

TO FINISH

Talk with your students about the importance of living like Christ, and encourage them to be an example of love, humility, faith and purity in all aspects of their lives.

Pray for one another, and intercede for the sick and needy. Sing some worship songs, and review the memory verse before saying goodbye.

Lesson 31
What do we believe?

Biblical References: 1 John 2:18-27; 4:1-6; 2 John 9.

Lesson Objective: That the pre-teens analyze and understand that the biblical doctrine of the deity of Jesus Christ is the only truth.

Memory Verse: *But if we walk in the light, as he is in the light, we have fellowship with one another, and the blood of Jesus, his Son, purifies us from all sin.* (1 John 1:7).

PREPARE YOURSELF TO TEACH!

Your students are discovering the diversity of ideas and thoughts that exist in the world. Whether at school, among friends or neighbors you will find that not everyone thinks the same way. Our students are bombarded by philosophies, ideologies and currents of thought that seek to distance them from the biblical truth, confusing their mind with ideas that are not helpful for their spiritual growth.

However, the Bible establishes the importance of recognizing the truth. In today's passage, John tells the Christians what to do with a group of false teachers and their wrong doctrines.

We know that young people are curious by nature. In their search for answers, they want to experiment and inquire for themselves. For that reason, it is important that, through this lesson, they learn that the Bible tells us the truth, and that all new ideologies and doctrines must be analyzed in light of the Bible's teachings.

It is likely that your students will have more questions than usual in this lesson. That is why we suggest that you prepare yourself to respond with clarity and, above all, with divine wisdom.

BIBLICAL COMMENTARY

1 John 2:18-27; 4:1-6. John knew that false teachers tried to introduce false doctrines into the church of Jesus Christ. Therefore, he warned Christians to be careful and stay away from these misconceptions. Many of those false teachers incorporated elements of the gospel into pagan beliefs or Jewish traditions. They often denied the total humanity or total deity of Christ, preaching other kinds of teachings that confused believers.

John gave advice to the early Christians, which are still valid for us. It is unfortunate that in our society, truth is a concept in disuse. In favor of the revolution of thought and the establishment of new ideologies, truth is distorted and altered to make it false. There are hundreds of sects that teach improbable concepts about Christ and salvation. That is why John also encourages us to seek the truth and get away from false doctrines.

The apostle tells us that we must "prove" those teachings in light of the Word of God. Any group, individual or movement that denies that Jesus is the Christ is wrong.

In 1 John 2:22-23, the writer clearly points out that whoever denies that Jesus is the Christ also denies the Father. John assures that the Father and the Son are one, and one can not be denied without denying the other.

Christians must stand firm in their faith, regardless of the currents and doctrines that govern this world. That is why it is very important that through this lesson, your students learn that the only truth is in Christ and in his Word.

LESSON DEVELOPMENT
True or false

Divide the group into two teams. As you read the following statements, your students should decide if they are true or false. Tell them that those who believe they are true must stand up, and those who think they are false stay sitting.

1. The most sleepy animal is the koala, which sleeps 22 hours a day. (True)
2. Scientists used the hippopotamus to do research, searching for the cure of leprosy. Infected hippos produce a substance known as lepromin that helps the patient in his recovery. (False)
3. The human skeleton is made up of 205 or 206 bones, according to the coccyx of each. More than half of them are in the hands and feet: 27 in each hand and 26 in each foot (106 in total). (True)
4. Mosquitoes have 47 teeth. (True)
5. A person's heart is the size of an apple. (False)

6. The largest crustacean in the world is the giant crab of Japan. Even though its body measures only 33 cm., its legs exceed five meters. (True)
7. The American continent is the most populated of all. (False)
8. The Caspian Sea, the Dead Sea and the Aral Sea are not seas, but lakes. In fact, the Caspian is the largest lake in the world. (True)
9. In Antarctica there is a great variety of birds and wild flowers. (False)
10. On April 23, International Book Day is celebrated, because on that day, in the year 1616, the two most famous writers of all time died: Miguel de Cervantes Saavedra and William Shakespeare. (True)

After finishing the game, ask them: How can you know if someone is telling you the truth? Allow them to respond, and then ask: How do you feel when you are not sure about something? How do you feel when you realize that someone lied to you and you thought they told you the truth? Listen to the answers. Then, tell them that in today's story we will learn what John said to some people who doubted the truth of Christ.

Different beliefs

Have students sit in a semicircle in front of the board, and ask them if they know what a "sect" is. Write the answers on the board, and explain that a sect is a religious group that has different beliefs than those that have been accepted through history. In general, sects grow because they have a leader with convincing power, but their beliefs are wrong.

Briefly explain the tragic end of some sects, such as the Davidics, led by David Koresh, who died in Waco, Texas.

Talk with them about the importance of choosing the right beliefs. God gave us the ability to choose freely. However, we must bear in mind that we are responsible for the decisions we make.

BIBLE STORY

We suggest that you seek the help of a young man from your congregation to present the role of John. Provide him in advance with the study material, and ask him to tell your students what John told the Christians in his letters (1 John 2:18-27; 4:1-6, 11-15; 2 John 9).

Have a table and chair to represent the place where John wrote. Explain to the class that they will receive a visit from a special person who will teach them what to do when confronted with false cults and doctrines.

ACTIVITIES
What do I believe?

Have the student find worksheet pages 115 and 116. They are to read the beliefs of the different religious groups, and put an X next to those that do not agree with God's Word.

In this activity, your students will see examples about the beliefs of some sects. Remember that the central point of this activity is not to criticize others for what they believe, but rather that preteens understand the importance of testing every teaching in light of the Word of God. In this way they can defend themselves against false doctrines and, with the help of the Lord, perhaps they can convince those who live in error.

The Apostle's Creed

This lesson will allow you to teach your students one of the most important statements of faith for Christians: the Apostle's Creed.

We suggest that you write it on a large piece of construction paper and place it in a visible place in the room. Explain it phrase by phrase, and let everyone repeat it with you. It is important that you clearly understand all the concepts that are expressed in this statement. You may need more than one class to explain it in its entirety, but it is necessary that the students know very well the foundations of their faith.

(You can find the Apostle's Creed in devotional reading No. 2 of the Hymnal Grace and Devotion).

TO FINISH

At the conclusion of this series of lessons, invite your students to confirm their faith in Jesus. Encourage them to study the Word of God to learn from it, but also to have solid arguments in defending their faith. Motivate them to stay firm and not give in to the pressure of people who want to confuse them.

This being the last lesson of the unit, recognize the effort of the students who learned the memory verse and other biblical passages. If possible, reward them with a treat or a bookmark for their Bible.

Encourage them to continue attending the classes, and mention the theme of the next unit that deals with a very important topic: the Holy Spirit.

THE HOLY SPIRIT

Biblical References: John 14:15-18; 14:5-26; 16:5-8; 16:7-15; Acts 1:3-8; 2:1-6; 6:1-15; 7:1, 51-60; 15:1-31; 2 Corinthians 1:21-22; 13:14.

Memory Verse: *But you will receive power when the Holy Spirit comes on you; and you will be my witnesses in Jerusalem, and in all Judea and Samaria, and to the ends of the earth.* (Acts 1:8).

THE PURPOSE OF THIS UNIT

This unit will help preteens to:

❖ Know the doctrine of the Trinity.

❖ Know that the Holy Spirit helps the children of God to live in holiness.

❖ Value the need to enjoy the power and guidance of the Holy Spirit in their daily life.

❖ Listen and obey the guidance of the Holy Spirit.

UNIT LESSONS

Lesson 32: Who is the Holy Spirit?

Lesson 33: The Holy Spirit teaches us

Lesson 34: The Holy Spirit guides us

Lesson 35: The Holy Spirit gives us power

WHY DO PRETEENS NEED THIS UNIT?

Maybe many of your students have heard about the Holy Spirit, some may even say something about him. However, very few understand clearly who he is and why he is important.

To experience healthy spiritual growth, young people need to understand the identity of the Holy Spirit and his role in the life of the believer. In this lesson, your students will study the doctrine of the Trinity. This teaching is part of a process of spiritual development that will help them better understand the essence and identity of the Christian and his relationship with God.

When they were little, their learning focused on God the Father. Then at the beginning of elementary school, the focus was Jesus Christ. Now, they will learn that the Holy Spirit is God with us.

They will also study some misconceptions that exist about the Trinity. For example, it is believed that the Holy Spirit is separate from the Father and the Son, or that it has less value than God. In addition, they will learn about the role of the Holy Spirit in the life of the believer. It is our prayer that through these lessons, you will teach your students that the Holy Spirit is real and wants to work in their lives to help them live in holiness.

The concept of the Trinity is complex and mysterious. Even so, there is a practical and easy way to understand the foundations of this doctrine. The most important principle for preadolescents is to know that God wants to be part of our life every day. God does this by living in us, through the Holy Spirit.

In summary, the fundamental truths about the Holy Spirit are the following:

· He is a person, not a thing. We must refer to him personally, not as an object.

· One of the tasks of the Holy Spirit is to help us understand the teachings of Jesus. The Holy Spirit will never teach anything contrary to the ministry of Christ, or to the testimony of the Bible.

· The Holy Spirit comforts us and helps us to have peace and harmony with God.

· The Holy Spirit gives us courage and power to have a life that pleases God. Before the Holy Spirit came, the disciples lived their faith in an inconsistent way. They were not willing to commit fully to the kingdom of God. However, after their experience with the Holy Spirit, they were transformed and received strength, courage and authority from God.

Who is the Holy Spirit?

Biblical References: John 14:16-18; 16:5-8; Acts 1:3-8; 2:1-6; 2 Corinthians 13:14.

Lesson Objective: That the pre-adolescents understand who the Holy Spirit is, and the importance that He has in our lives.

Memory Verse: *But you will receive power when the Holy Spirit comes on you; and you will be my witnesses in Jerusalem, and in all Judea and Samaria, and to the ends of the earth.* (Acts 1:8).

PREPARE YOURSELF TO TEACH!

Human beings have a natural inclination towards the spiritual. For this reason, thousands of people seek to satisfy that deep inner need with different religious doctrines and practices. As a consequence, many end up with wounds in their soul that can hardly be cured.

However, the children of God receive a different treatment. God has provided us with a Comforter; and not only that, but He has given us a teacher, guide and counselor: the Holy Spirit.

In the Old Testament, communion with God was through obedience to the law. In the New Testament, the first disciples experienced communion with God through the company of Jesus Christ, who was at their side. But now, neither of these two ways is available to Christians.

But Romans 8:26-27 says that:

a. the Spirit helps us in our weakness,

b. intercedes for us with unspeakable groans and,

c. intercedes for the saints according to the will of God.

Knowing who the Holy Spirit is and how he works in our life is the foundation of our trust and hope. Without adequate knowledge of this, God becomes unreachable and incomprehensible.

In this lesson, preteens will learn that God is with us through the Holy Spirit. The physical presence of God was with the first disciples in the person of Jesus. Now God is with us through the Holy Spirit.

BIBLICAL COMMENTARY

John 14:16-17. In this passage Jesus told his disciples that soon his physical presence would no longer be with them. However, he promised that he would not leave them alone, because the Father would send them "another Comforter". The word that is translated as "other" is very important, because it contains the idea of "another of the same class." Therefore, the Holy Spirit continues the ministry and message of Jesus.

This passage speaks of one of the primary roles of the Holy Spirit: He is the Spirit of truth that will live in the hearts of believers.

2 Corinthians 13:14. Paul reminds the believers in Corinth that God works in them and through them to fulfill his will. The Corinthian church had gone through times of difficulty. However, God wanted to continue ministering to them through the Holy Spirit. This beautiful blessing reminds us of the abundant presence and concern of God for his children in the midst of difficulties.

LESSON DEVELOPMENT

After welcoming your students, ask them what they know about the Holy Spirit. Listen to their answers, and read aloud the explanation on page 117 of the student worksheet. Divide the class into pairs or small groups and give them five minutes to answer the four questions, based on what they understood from the reading.

When everyone is finished, review the answers and make sure they are all correct. We suggest that you prepare yourself in prayer and study of the Word so that you can explain with truth and clarity the subject of the Holy Spirit.

Three people in one?

This activity will help you better understand the idea of God the Father, God the Son and God the Holy Spirit.

Get different types of hats (for example: a construction hardhat, an athlete's cap, a chef's hat, etc.). Ask a volunteer to come forward and put one on his head. Meanwhile, ask your students: Do you believe that a person can do different things? For example, can a cook play a sport? Can a construction worker cook? Explain that just as a person can have several titles (as a doctor and as a parent), so God, Jesus and the Spirit have different names but is one person.

BIBLE STORY

Gather your students for this activity. Ask the guys to look up John 14:15-18, and the girls to look up John 16:5-8.

Allow time for both groups to discuss what they understand about the passage and write their conclusions. Based on these, tell the biblical story.

ACTIVITIES

How does the Holy Spirit help us?

This activity will help students better understand some of the functions of the Holy Spirit. Ask them to look closely at the pictures on page 118. Then divide the class into four groups. Give three questions to each group, and give them time to answer.

Then, ask each group to present their answers. Stay alert to help resolve any questions that arise during the activity.

Help for students

Ask the class to stay in their groups to discuss the cases on page 119 and answer the questions.

After they discuss their conclusions, invite them to accept the help that the Holy Spirit offers each one so that they may live the Christian life. If you see fit, lead them in prayer, asking for the filling of the Holy Spirit in their lives.

What would the Holy Spirit do?

Explain to the kids that they will have a special task to do at home that week. The student worksheet should be taken home to do the activity on page 120.

Tell them that if they have questions, to consult the study passages. Remind them that they must bring the completed activity to review in the next class.

Power from on high

Tell them that this time they will begin learning a new Bible verse, Acts 1:8: "But you will receive power, when the Holy Spirit has come upon you, and you will be my witnesses in Jerusalem, in all Judea, in Samaria, and

to the end of the earth. " Explain that this passage is closely related to the theme of study of this unit: the Holy Spirit.

We suggest the following activity to help your students become familiar with the text of the unit.

Memorization competition

Read the Bible verse aloud a couple of times. Then, divide the class into two teams and give them paper and pencil. Place a table in the center, and ask the teams to each place their paper at the ends.

The goal is for each member of the team to individually run to the table and write a word of the verse. Then he will pass the pencil to the next partner in line.

If he does not know the next word, he will have to run to the table and place a question mark in the space he had. The next participant can delete the question mark and write the missing word. The first team to write the whole verse without any errors will be the winner.

TO FINISH

Ask a volunteer to write prayer requests on the board, and assign several students to pray for each one. Then, conclude by asking the Lord to help the students know the Holy Spirit better. Do a final review of the Memory verse.

The Holy Spirit teaches us

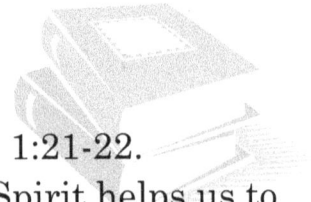

Biblical References: John 14:5-26; 16:7-15; 2 Corinthians 1:21-22.

Lesson Objective: That the students know that the Holy Spirit helps us to understand the teachings of Jesus.

Memory Verse: *But you will receive power when the Holy Spirit comes on you; and you will be my witnesses in Jerusalem, and in all Judea and Samaria, and to the ends of the earth.* (Acts 1:8).

PREPARE YOURSELF TO TEACH!

Throughout their academic life, students will meet a wide variety of teachers, all with different methods and teaching habits. Some they will remember for their kindness and affection, others for their rigidity, and others for their knowledge.

However, all are fallible; none has the absolute truth. Even the great scientists, pedagogues and philosophers made mistakes that made their followers question their teachings.

Today, there are also "false teachers" who pollute the mind and heart of man. Among them are television, sects, existentialist ideologies, etc. However, there is an infallible teacher who gives us wise and loving instruction: the Holy Spirit.

In this lesson it is important that your students analyze who is doing the teaching. They must realize that the only one who can teach us the truth is the Holy Spirit. The reason is that he teaches only the words and principles Jesus taught.

At this stage of their life, it is common for youngsters to rebel against the good teachings of their parents and Bible class teachers. Many times they prefer to learn from their friends, neighbors or school teachers. It is very important that you emphasize the great work that the Holy Spirit does in our hearts to help us live out the teachings of Jesus, our best teacher.

BIBLICAL COMMENTARY

John 14:5-26; 16:7-15. In this passage we read that Jesus instructed his disciples before his death, and promised that he would not leave them alone. He would send to them the Comforter, or Holy Spirit, who would help them know the truth and accompany them in their ministry.

He also told them that the Holy Spirit would help them remember his teachings and stand firm in the faith.

Through this passage, we understand that God sent the Holy Spirit to help the believer "fight the good fight". He works through our conscience to help us resist temptation. However, we must understand that our conscience is not the same as the Holy Spirit. The conscience, when ignored, becomes negligent and the person can deliberately disobey the words of Jesus without feeling guilty. The Holy Spirit will never treat us with a tone of condemnation; His ministry is gentle, but firm, to remind us of Jesus' teachings.

2 Corinthians 1:21-22. The Word tells us that Christians receive the anointing of the Holy Spirit. This means that they consecrate themselves to God and dedicate themselves to his service. Through the Holy Spirit, Christians receive power to live in holiness and be witnesses of Christ. Through him, God puts the seal of ownership on us.

The Spirit represents the wonderful presence of Jesus among us. Just as Jesus Christ represented the attributes and essence of the Father, the Holy Spirit represents the attributes, teachings and essence of Jesus.

LESSON DEVELOPMENT

Start the lesson by asking your students how they did last week, and how the Holy Spirit helped them make a decision in their daily lives. Let some tell of their experiences.

Then, ask them to find page 121 of their worksheet and do the activity: What do they teach me? After listening to their answers, tell them that every day we learn in different ways (for example, through our parents, teachers, family members, our own mistakes, books, television, friends, etc.). Today's lesson tells us about someone who wants to teach us something very special.

Teachers?

For this activity you will need magazines or newspapers to cut out, cardboard and glue. Ask your students to look in the magazines or photographs that exemplify the different means by which people receive teaching: the classroom, television, internet, famous people, books, politics, etc.

When they have found a good number, give them time to stick them on the cardboard and explain what each one represents.

As they work, explain that we are all exposed to a great many teachings, many of them contrary to the Word of God.

Today we will learn about the only teacher who teaches us only the truth, who wants to help us grow in our spiritual life.

BIBLE STORY

Use the activity on page 121 to reflect on. Explain the words they do not understand and use the following activity so they can read and reflect on today's Bible story.

Organize your students in three teams. Each one should analyze a biblical passage and answer the questions on page 122. Afterwards, each team should present their answers to the group and conclude the activity by noting on the board the important functions of the Holy Spirit in the life of each Christian.

ACTIVITIES

True or false

Before the class, make two signs. One that says "FALSE" and the other "TRUE". Glue them on opposite walls of the room before your students arrive. Explain that you will read some statements and they should stand under the sign they think is right. Each one must be prepared to answer why he/she chose that answer.

1. The Holy Spirit reminds me that I am part of the family of God. (True)
2. The Holy Spirit scares me.
3. The Holy Spirit helps me realize when I do something wrong. (True)
4. The Holy Spirit is the same as my conscience. (False)
5. The Holy Spirit is only for pastors, missionaries and church leaders. (False)
6. The Holy Spirit helps me understand the Word of God. (True)
7. The Holy Spirit is in all people, even if they are not Christian. (False)
8. The Holy Spirit is the best counselor. (True)
9. The Holy Spirit helps me lie to someone when the truth can hurt their feelings. (False)
10. The Holy Spirit is a member of the Trinity: God the Father, God the Son and God Holy Spirit. (True)

What's going on?

Have students look at page 123. Give them time to read the stories and answer what the Holy Spirit can teach us in those situations.

Give them paper so that everyone can write their answers. Then, ask them to exchange them so that another partner can read them out loud. After listening to all the answers, discuss to reach a general conclusion and write it on the worksheets.

TO FINISH

Before saying goodbye, ask your students to make a list on page 124 of everything they want the Holy Spirit to teach them.

This activity will be personal, and only the owner of the activity sheet will know everything he wrote down on his list. Review the memory verse, and conclude by guiding them in prayer.

The Holy Spirit guides us

Biblical References: John 16:12-14; Acts 15:1-31.

Lesson Objective: That the students understand that it is important to allow the Holy Spirit to guide our life.

Memory Verse: *But you will receive power when the Holy Spirit comes on you; and you will be my witnesses in Jerusalem, and in all Judea and Samaria, and to the ends of the earth. (Acts 1:8).*

PREPARE YOURSELF TO TEACH!

It is common for some of the kids in the class to show an attitude of self-sufficiency. However, they really need other people to guide them in the important decisions of their life. When they are alone, they act on impulse and without taking external factors into account.

The role models they decide to follow will be crucial for their training.

You will have noticed that at this stage, your students want to enjoy their freedom; they do not want to hear comments or suggestions from anyone, especially if it is from their parents and teachers. Therefore, they need to discover in the Word of God that the Holy Spirit is the best guide. He is reliable and will help them in their spiritual development.

In this stage of emotional and spiritual immaturity of young people, the guidance of the Holy Spirit will be decisive.

BIBLICAL COMMENTARY

John 16:12-14. In these verses Jesus emphasizes the function of the Holy Spirit as a guide. Jesus said that the Holy Spirit is the Spirit of truth and that, through him, Christians can continue to learn biblical truths.

Jesus continues his teaching ministry through the work of the Holy Spirit in believers. Many claim to live under the leadership of the Holy Spirit, but continue to live in direct contradiction to what Jesus taught.

Later, this passage shows us that God did not stop guiding people when Jesus left this earth, or when the last book of the Bible was written. God continues to speak to believers through the Holy Spirit.

Acts 15:1-31. As the church grew, the Gentiles also heard the gospel message. The term "Gentiles" included everyone who was not Jewish by birth. When these people began to convert to the gospel, many Jews opposed because of their ingrained customs, to the point that many Gentiles had to convert to Judaism to become Christians.

Should a Gentile submit to circumcision and all Jewish laws and rituals in order to be a member of the church? Should a gentile become a Jew to be a Christian? Could a Gentile be part of the church simply because of their faith in Jesus Christ?

These were not the only questions that the first believers were asking. Orthodox Jews were forbidden to interact with Gentiles. If they became part of the church, could the Jews interact with them?

To answer these questions, Paul and Barnabas appealed to the apostles and elders of Jerusalem. That decision depended on whether they opened the doors of the gospel to non-Jews, or whether they would convert Christianity into a small Jewish sect.

The solution was not easy. Was the grace of God only for certain people, or for all? The Holy Spirit led the apostles to solve this problem.

The Jerusalem Council decided that there would be no difference between Jews and Gentiles. Therefore, we can trust in the guidance and direction of the Holy Spirit, who is the best Counselor.

LESSON DEVELOPMENT

Start the class with this question: How many would like to drive some type of transport? Listen to their answers and then add that, just as every vehicle of transportation needs a driver or guide to get to a place, also we human beings need someone to guide us on the right path.

Who guides your life?

Give half a piece of paper and a pencil to each person. Ask them to write down the five most important influences that guide their lives. Then, ask them to read their answers out loud, and write the ones that have been repeated many times on the board.

Ask your students: Why do you think these influences are good for you? Listen to the answers. Then, mention that in today's class you will learn who is the only one who can guide us with wisdom.

Can you follow these instructions?

Open the student worksheets to page 125. Ask a volunteer to read the instructions aloud, while others try to follow the instructions to perform the action.

Answers:

1. Breathe through your mouth.
2. Wink with your right eye.
3. Bend over and using your pinkie finger of your dominant hand, point at your left big toe.

4. Bend your knees repeatedly while holding your arms out in front of you.

After trying to do all four activities, explain that it is often difficult to follow directions when they are very complicated.

For that we need a guide to help us. In today's class we will learn who is the guide that God sent to help us overcome the trials of life.

BIBLE STORY

Ask someone to read the Bible passage in Acts 15:1-31 while everyone else follows along. Then talk about the problem for which the first council of the Christian church in Jerusalem met. Divide the board into two columns: in one write the arguments of the Jews, and in the other the arguments of the Gentiles. Next, look on page 127 for the agreements of the council and how the Holy Spirit intervened.

Holy Spirit, guide me!

After learning how the Holy Spirit intervenes in the lives of believers to guide them, it is time to reflect on their personal experience. Give them time to individually answer the questions on page 128 and ponder whether their life is being led by the Holy Spirit or by their own desires. Then ask some to tell what they wrote. End by repeating John 16:13.

TO FINISH

Conclude with a prayer of thanksgiving to God for sending us his Holy Spirit, who teaches and guides us. Remind them that in order to know what God's will is for their life, they should read the Bible and pray every day. Review the Memory verse, and dismiss everyone by singing some praise songs to God.

notes

Lesson 35

The Holy Spirit gives us power

Biblical References: Acts 1:8; 6:1-15; 7:1, 51-60.

Lesson Objective: That the pre-teens appreciate the power that the Holy Spirit gives to Christians to proclaim the message of salvation and defend their faith.

Memory Verse: *But you will receive power when the Holy Spirit comes on you; and you will be my witnesses in Jerusalem, and in all Judea and Samaria, and to the ends of the earth (Acts 1:8).*

PREPARE YOURSELF TO TEACH!

It is impressive to observe what today's society is willing to do to obtain power. In short, our society is hungry for power. From all social levels, people struggle to dominate the lives of others and thus have control of situations. No doubt, your students have experienced it, or at least they have seen it in others.

In this lesson, your students will learn that God gives power and courage to Christians through the Holy Spirit. However, this power is completely different from what the world aspires to, because it does not seek its own benefit but that of others; it does not destroy to get its own way, but gives in so that God may fulfill His will.

BIBLICAL COMMENTARY

Acts 1:8. In this verse we find Jesus' promise to send the Holy Spirit to believers. He would empower them to be witnesses and perform miracles. Jesus knew that his disciples could not be witnesses by their own strength, so he asked them to wait for "the promise of the Father." As described in this Biblical passage, the disciples were to be witnesses not only in Jerusalem, but even to the last corner of the earth.

The Greek word for "witness" is "martus," the same word used for "martyr." A witness must be willing to be a martyr, and this kind of strength can only come from the Holy Spirit.

Acts 6:1-15. When the church began to grow, a dispute arose between the Greeks and the Hebrews over the distribution of help for the needy. The Greeks complained because their widows were not looked after. The apostles did not want to neglect preaching, so they prayed that the Lord would help them choose special people for the task. Therefore, they appointed seven deacons to take care of spiritual and material needs. These men were to be filled with the Holy Spirit.

This reminds us that the Holy Spirit transforms ordinary people into powerful witnesses of Christ.

Acts 7:1, 51-60. The story of Stephen, the first Christian martyr, is a clear sign of the power of the Holy Spirit in the believer. Although in reality it seems a contradiction, because Stephen died helpless at the hands of an angry mob. However, his heart and spirit were strengthened and full of power and love.

In this passage there are three key points that we must highlight:

1. The secret of Stephen's strength was his total dependence on Christ. This kind of power can only come from the Holy Spirit.

2. Stephen followed the example of Jesus. Instead of attacking his aggressors, he prayed that God would forgive them.

3. We learn what it means to be witnesses of Christ regardless of the consequences. The power of the Holy Spirit was working in Stephen, even at the moment of his death.

LESSON DEVELOPMENT

The Memory verse will serve as an introduction to this last lesson. In this verse we find the confirmation of the promise that Christ made to his followers: that he would send the Holy Spirit.

Write the text on the board, and ask the preteens if they have already received that power. Based on the answers, explain that in today's lesson you will learn what it means to live filled with the Spirit of God.

What makes it work?

For this activity you will need the following: a radio or stereo, a small lamp and an appliance.

Turn on each of the items, and then ask the preteens what it is that makes them work. Listen to your answers. Then, explain that just as many objects need some kind of power, i.e., electricity, wind or a fuel to function, so human beings need power to face the challenges of life. In our society, power is important, and some people misuse it. However, God promised that He would give us a different kind of power, as we will learn in the biblical story.

Could you do this?

To better understand the role of the power of the Holy Spirit in the lives of Christians, we will reflect on two real-life stories. One happened in Jerusalem in the first century, and the other in South America in this last century.

Open the student's worksheets to page 129, and allow time for the preteens to silently read the story of Jim Elliot.

When everyone is finished, discuss these two questions: What enabled Elizabeth Elliot to do what she did? What do you think you would have done in that situation?

Allow everyone to participate and write the conclusions in the worksheet.

BIBLE STORY

Divide the class into pairs or small groups, and assign each one of the questions on page 130. To find the answers, ask them to read Acts 6:8-15; 7:1, 51-60. Each group must appoint a representative who will be the one to give the answer to the rest of the class. Be alert to correct any incorrect answers and supplement the information when necessary.

ACTIVITIES

I saw it

Tell your students that, imagining they had witnessed Stephen's death, write a letter telling a friend or family member what happened. Explain that they should write the details about how they felt when they saw Stephen unjustly accused and dying at the hands of the Pharisees.

Then, allow some to read their letters. Encourage them to follow Stephen's example and remain steadfast in their faith, even when the circumstances are adverse.

The Holy Spirit is ...

Give the preteens a piece of cardboard and pencils. Ask them to draw a picture, or write a thought about what the Holy Spirit represents for their lives, after having studied this series of lessons.

Prepare a wall to make a mural collage of their drawings, and if you wish, invite parents to see the work their children did.

TO FINISH

Form a prayer circle and pray for each of your students. Pray for the Holy Spirit to fill them, empower them, and guide them to live the Christian life. If any of the students haven't yet accepted Christ as their personal Savior and Lord, it would be a good time for you to invite them to do so.

Encourage your class to trust and depend on the guidance of the Holy Spirit at all times in their lives.

Remind them that the next class will begin the study of a new unit titled "Lessons We Learn from Three Kings."

LESSONS WE LEARN FROM THREE KINGS

Biblical References: 1 Samuel 8-12; 13; 15; 18-19; 28; 31; 2 Samuel 11-12; Psalm 51; 1 Kings 3; 4:29-34; 9:1-9; 11:1-13.

Unit Verse: *And now, Israel, what does the Lord your God ask of you but to fear the Lord your God, to walk in obedience to him, to love him, to serve the Lord your God with all your heart and with all your soul* (Deuteronomy 10:12).

THE PURPOSE OF THIS UNIT

This unit will help preteens:

- To understand that in their relationship with God, respect, obedience, service and love are foundational.
- To identify the causes that impede their spiritual growth.
- To evaluate whether their decisions reflect obedience or disobedience of God.
- To seek the forgiveness of their sins and the restoration of their relationship with God.

Lessons from the unit

Lesson 36: Israel has a king

Lesson 37: The king disobeys God

Lesson 38: From bad to worse

Lesson 39: Can there be a good king?

Lesson 40: The fall of a wise king

Why do preteens need the teaching of this unit?

As they grow up, preteens tend to relate to more people: friends, classmates, teachers, etc. Many of these relationships are firm and lasting, others are weak and fleeting.

Your students begin to understand what it means to maintain and care for a friendship. They know that it is important to know the person and accept them with their defects and virtues. However, since our relationship with God is the most important, they must understand that they also need to know Him better. For that reason it is so important that they study the Bible and pray.

Jesus' conversation with Nicodemus (John 3) shows us how to start a right relationship with God. The church understands that "being born again" is admitting that we have sinned (repentance) and accepting Christ as our Lord.

Many biblical passages, both Old Testament and New Testament, teach us how to maintain and strengthen our relationship with God. Deuteronomy 10:12 provides four elements that help us fulfill this purpose: fear of God (honor and respect), obedience (walking in his ways), love and service.

For there to be a harmonious relationship, we need these four elements together. For example, if people follow rules but do not obey God, they become legalistic like the Pharisees. If one says he loves God but does not respect His commandments, his faith is based only on feelings. On the other hand, if he is only dedicated to service, he simply becomes a charitable person. It is impossible to honor and respect God if we do not obey, love and serve. Anything else is superficial religion. But, by combining the four elements, there is a balance between attitudes and actions. We serve and obey God because we love and respect him.

These lessons tell us about the time of the kings, from Saul to Solomon. In each story your students will evaluate to what extent Saul, David and Solomon met the four requirements, and how this influenced their lives.

Lesson 36
Israel has a king

Biblical References: 1 Samuel 8-12.

Lesson Objective: That pre-teens learn the four elements that are necessary to maintain a good relationship with God.

Memory Verse: *And now, Israel, what does the Lord your God ask of you but to fear the Lord your God, to walk in obedience to him, to love him, to serve the Lord your God with all your heart and with all your soul* (Deuteronomy 10:12).

PREPARE YOURSELF TO TEACH!

The most important decision in the lives of people is to accept Jesus Christ as their Savior and Lord. However, the Christian life does not end with the forgiveness of sins; it is a continuous relationship that needs to be enriched and strengthened.

The Bible tells us clearly what God expects from his children: respect, love, obedience and service. These requirements were established for the people of Israel, but they are still valid for us. When the Christian fails in an area of their life, it is easy to see a change in his or her relationship with God.

Pre-teens learn easily through the experiences of other people. Therefore, through the stories of these biblical characters, talk to them about the importance of obeying, loving, respecting and serving God. Since these men also failed, teach the class to recognize their mistakes and decide how they will avoid falling into sin so as not to ruin their relationship with God.

BIBLICAL COMMENTARY

1 Samuel 8-12. For more than 400 years, Israel was special among the nations for being a theocratic people. That is, their government was governed by absolute divine authority. God chose men and women to be judges, a function that included military leadership, as well as legal and moral authority. The judges were the representatives of God, but he was the King of Israel. This ended in the time of Samuel, about a thousand years before Christ.

In the Hebrew manuscripts, 1 and 2 Samuel was a single book, like 1 and 2 Kings, and 1 and 2 Chronicles. These books together document the beginning and fall of the monarchy in Israel. The first seven chapters of 1 Samuel narrate the transition between the era of judges and the monarchy.

Samuel was the last judge of Israel, and the one who anointed the first two kings. Therefore, it was an important link between the two periods. He warned the people about the consequences of asking for a king; but led by God, he listened to the request of the people and helped to establish the monarchy.

The leaders of Israel gave Samuel three reasons why they wanted a king: (1) Samuel was an old man and his children were corrupt. (2) They thought that appointing a king would avoid future military problems - it is more than evident that they had forgotten the miraculous victories under the leadership of judges like Deborah and Gideon. Finally, (3) they wanted to be like other nations (8:5). God told Samuel that the people were not rejecting him, but rejecting God himself as their king.

God would not allow them to be like the other nations because Israel was the people of his covenant. Not even the king would have absolute authority in Israel; his powers were strictly limited (see Deuteronomy 17:14-20). The monarchy in Israel would be theocratic, that is, the power of the king would be under the direction and control of God.

DEVELOPMENT OF THE LESSON

Welcome your students, and tell them that in this unit they will study the life of the first kings of Israel. Remind them that they must bring their Bible and arrive on time to participate in the learning activities. Start the class with prayer. Then ask a volunteer to help you distribute the worksheets.

What makes a friendship last?

Divide the class into groups of three or four students and ask each group to name a secretary. Instruct them to find page 131 of their worksheets and discuss the characteristics of a lasting friendship (for example: honesty, kindness, compassion, forgiveness, love, etc.). Give them time to write the answers on their sheets. Ask the secretary of each group to read their answers and write them on the board.

Explain that for a friendship to be lasting, there must be love, respect, loyalty and understanding. The same happens in our relationship with God. If we want to be his friends and learn from him, we must know him more and love him with all our heart.

Kings

For this activity you will need cardboard, colored markers, glue and illustrations of crowns, thrones, scepters, palaces, kings, etc.

Put the materials on a table for your students to make a mural about kings. As you work, ask them to name some characteristics and functions of kings.

After placing the finished mural on the wall, tell them that during this unit they will study the history of three important kings of Israel.

BIBLE STORY

Read the biblical study passages in advance, noting the important facts on cards to keep them handy. Explain to the class the form of government that the Israelites had before becoming a monarchy.

Give them time to read the biblical passages and say in their own words what they understood. Explain the difficult concepts, emphasizing that the Israelites, wanting to be like the other nations, despised the authority of God and preferred to be ruled by a human being like them.

ACTIVITIES

Find the way

Ask your pre-teens to open their Bible in Deuteronomy 10:12 and work on the activity on page 132. There they must find the way, following the biblical text, and circle the four requirements to have a good relationship with God.

Attitudes

Have the class find page 133. Ask the guys to answer the questions that correspond to the attitude of Israel, while the girls look at the biblical passages that relate to the attitude of Saul. Then, both groups should compare their results, and verify that they agree with what was studied in the biblical story.

Enduring friendship

We suggest that for this occasion you invite your best friend to tell the group a story about your friendship. This will help preteens understand better that a relationship is built on the foundation of trust, respect, loyalty and love. Tell them that just as they want to spend time and have fun with their friends, they should strive to maintain a relationship of love and friendship with God.

How to start?

On page 134 of the student's worksheet they will find the steps to begin a relationship of love and friendship with God. Ask if any of them wants to know God more and live according to his commandments. If so, lead them in a prayer. Then, explain the importance of prayer and the study of the Word to get closer to the Lord and have a more intimate relationship with him.

TO FINISH

Encourage your students to respect, obey, love and serve God every day. Sing some praises and study the Memory verse of this unit. We suggest that you write it on a piece of cardboard and place it in a visible place in the room to remember it continuously. Intercede for prayer requests and remind them that their attendance is very important.

The king disobeys God

Biblical References: 1 Samuel 13; 15.

Lesson Objective: That the preadolescents understand that obedience to God is the best sacrifice.

Memory Verse: *And now, Israel, what does the Lord your God ask of you but to fear the Lord your God, to walk in obedience to him, to love him, to serve the Lord your God with all your heart and with all your soul* (Deuteronomy 10:12).

PREPARE YOURSELF TO TEACH!

It is not strange that preadolescents observe that "good" people disobey God and apparently do not suffer consequences. On the other hand, whether by instinct or by imitation, when people do something bad, they try to do something good in compensation. But such a tendency is misleading because it gives a false sense of security. In addition, it is common for many to think: "After all, there is always someone worse than me."

Good works, even great sacrifices, do not erase disobedience. Disobeying God is a sin and only God can forgive that. No good work, however many, can compensate for sin. However, God is willing to forgive the one who asks and believes in him. Once he forgives the person, he may guide him to make restitution, but we should not confuse that with earning forgiveness, which is a gift from God. Restitution is the response that the person whom God forgave offers out of love.

BIBLICAL COMMENTARY

1 Samuel 13. The people had asked for a king and God had granted it to them. Now they must suffer the consequences of their decision.

Although Israel had a king, their government was a theocratic monarchy because God was still the supreme authority for the king's power came from Him, and He demanded that the king of Israel obey His laws.

Saul's first act of disobedience was to assume the priestly role by offering a burnt offering in Gilgal. He was concerned to see that the Philistines were meeting and Samuel was not coming. His army, hidden and fearful, began to disperse upon seeing the large enemy army. And because Saul did not want to go out and fight without having offered a sacrifice to God, he took the role of priest, thus violating the laws.

Other cultures used to combine the roles of king and priest. Some pagan kings were supreme leaders, both politically and religiously. We find an antecedent in Genesis 14:18, when Melchizedek, king of Salem, acted as a priest of God to bless Abram. But that did not happen in Israel anymore. The priestly function was reserved for the Levites (Exodus 39-40), and Saul was of the tribe of Benjamin. His disobedience to the law showed that, indifferent to God's command, he depended on his army and military dominance.

1 Samuel 15. Saul's second great error was to disobey the order that God gave him through Samuel: destroy the Amalekites completely. Perhaps this order sounds cruel today, but Saul did not protest because it was common then. Otherwise, there was an enemy that sought revenge again and again. Although Saul accepted the order, out of selfishness and greed he did not want to waste the best cattle, nor the opportunity to show off the Amalekite king as a trophy for all Israel.

When Samuel rebuked Saul for his disobedience, he lied when he said, "But I did obey the Lord. I went on the mission the Lord assigned me. I completely destroyed the Amalekites and brought back Agag their king. The soldiers took sheep and cattle from the plunder, the best of what was devoted to God, in order to sacrifice them to the Lord your God at Gilgal" (15:20-21).

Samuel answered, "Does the Lord delight in burnt offerings and sacrifice as much as

in obeying the Lord?" (15:22). No sacrifice, however many, can replace obedience. This action ultimately cost Saul his kingdom.

The tragedy in Saul's story was not that he lost the throne, but that he decided to disobey God. His reign began with power and divine anointing, but ended in shame.

DEVELOPMENT OF THE LESSON

Review

On different colored paper write in disorder the four requirements necessary to maintain a correct relationship with God. Then ask the students to decipher the words. Example: ROMONRHI (honor him), OLMEHVI, (love him), EOIBMYH (obey him), EMVRISEH (serve him).

Consequences of disobedience

Divide the board into two columns. Over one column write as a title "Disobedience", and in the other "Consequences." Make a list of acts of disobedience of God that preteens often commit (for example: disobeying parents, not doing homework, missing school without parents knowing, taking something that does not belong to them, lying, etc.).

Then, allow the children to come forward and write the consequences of each action in the second column.

Explain that disobedience is sin and that it always has negative consequences. In today's story they will learn about a king who God had chosen to serve him, but he decided to disobey Him.

BIBLE STORY

Read the study passages in advance: 1 Samuel 13:8-15; 15:1-29. Your students have that passage in the form of a theater script in their worksheets, page 135. Choose five volunteers to read the text in dramatization form. (You can provide costumes to for the characters if you want.) Ask the rest of the class to observe the dramatization very carefully to determine if Saul met the requirements to have a right relationship with God.

When they are finished, explain that God wanted the Israelites to honor Him with their whole being and to be obedient. However, the king decided to follow his own desires and not listen to the voice of God. Make some comparisons with the attitudes of preadolescents regarding obedience and respect for the commandments of the Lord.

ACTIVITIES

And now what do I do?

For your students to relate the biblical story to what is going on around them, read the stories of Paula and Rick on page 137 of the student's worksheet, and talk about what happened. Actually, are Paula and Rick repentant? Does God like what they did? Are they repaying the damage?

Emphasize the importance of restitution when we have done something wrong. Restitution does not do away with our guilt, but it shows our repentance and desire to make amends for our misconduct.

What does God want us to do?

Ask some volunteers to read the dialogues on page 138 of the student worksheet. Then, talk about it. Emphasize that the only thing we can do to restore our relationship with God is admit that we have sinned, repent and ask for forgiveness.

Ask your students: What did Saul do after he disobeyed God? After listening to their answers, explain that Saul tried to protect himself by telling a lie. Then, he blamed the town, but he did not admit his fault.

When we sin, God is willing to forgive us if we repent from the heart and seek his forgiveness with humility.

TO FINISH

Conclude with a time of reflection. Some of these questions may be useful:

1. Have you done something wrong that you should talk to God about?

2. Are you trying to fix a problem in your own way or get out of some mess you got into?

Form a circle, and lead them in a prayer of confession, restitution and thanksgiving. Encourage them to approach the Lord with confidence to continue learning from his Word.

From bad to worse

Biblical References:1 Samuel 18-19; 28; 31.

Lesson Objective: That pre-teens understand that disobedience to God carries severe consequences.

Memory Verse: *And now, Israel, what does the Lord your God ask of you but to fear the Lord your God, to walk in obedience to him, to love him, to serve the Lord your God with all your heart and with all your soul* (Deuteronomy 10:12).

PREPARE YOURSELF TO TEACH!

Modern societies face an alarming and increasingly common problem: stress in preadolescents. Although they do not express it openly, they live in anguish, worried and confused by family problems, school pressures and the influence of the media. This often leads to rebellious behavior.

For preadolescents, bad behavior is common. They do not understand that they are establishing patterns of behavior for the future, and that small acts of disobedience can become major problems. They are not aware of the damage or the consequences, because television gives a distorted perspective of the consequences, presenting sin as something acceptable and even desirable.

The story of Saul shows us very clearly the results of disobedience and the consequences that it entails in the long term. Through this story, preteens will understand that their decision to obey God is fundamental to maintaining a loving relationship with the Lord.

BIBLICAL COMMENTARY

1 Samuel 18-19; 28; 31. Saul was the man God had chosen to be the first king of Israel. Unfortunately, because of his disobedience, his relationship with God was severed, and he lost his peace of mind and his kingdom.

If Saul had faithfully served God, his end would have been different, and perhaps his family would have established a great dynasty. However, Saul broke his covenant with God. Again and again he disobeyed the divine word and, when problems arose, he blamed others.

The final chapter of his life came when he had to face his former enemies: the Philistines. Samuel had died, and Saul, filled with fear, tried desperately to seek help to resolve the conflict.

In those days, it was common for kings to consult oracles or sages before waging a battle. Some pagan priests killed animals and examined their entrails for signs of the future.

Divination and witchcraft were forbidden in Israel. God provided his people with the direction they needed, speaking to them through prayer, prophets and priests, dreams, or the Urim and Thummim. None of these methods gave Saul the answer he wanted. Finally, disobeying what Deuteronomy 18:9-11 teaches, he went to a fortune-teller's house and asked him to call Samuel (1 Samuel 28:11).

The response Saul received was discouraging, confirming once again that God had abandoned him. Samuel foretold the defeat of the Israelites, and that Saul and his sons would die.

As Samuel said, the Philistines defeated the Israelites the next day, wounded Saul and killed his three sons. Instead of facing capture and subsequent torture by his enemies, Saul was killed with his own sword. The first king of Israel had died as a result of his disobedience and rebellion.

DEVELOPMENT OF THE LESSON

On the blackboard, or on a large piece of paper, write the following sentence: "Practice makes us perfect." Then, place on the table some objects that represent skills that require constant practice; for example, a paper with math exercises; a musical instrument; a garbage bag or a small trash can, representing the household chores, etc. Then, ask your students to form a circle, and stand in the center with a medium ball. Throw it to several of them and ask them to throw it back to you. Then, ask them if they could improve on throwing and catching the ball if they practiced every day. Then ask them the following questions:

- How often do you practice math exercises?
- How often do you practice playing an instrument?
- How often do you do household chores, such as taking out trash, sweeping the yard, washing or drying dishes, etc.?

Explain that when we practice something, we perfect that capacity and become better, for better or for worse. People who practice disobedience continuously become experts in doing so. In the Bible we find the case of a man who began to disobey God and the consequences were disastrous.

What's going on?

Distribute the student worksheets and ask to find page 139. Choose seven students to read the phrases in the boxes. Then talk about Mark's behavior and ask them: Do you think Mark can be a good friend? Listen to their answers. Then, explain that although each separate incident seems unimportant, if the behavior is recurrent, people will think that person is dishonest and will not trust him/her.

In today's story, we will learn about a man who disobeyed God many times, suffering sad consequences for his actions.

BIBLE STORY

For this occasion, we suggest that you ask two young people in advance to help you present the dialogue on page 140 of the student worksheet. Get tunics, swords or soldiers' costumes to make the representation more real.

Do a general review with your students of the history of Saul, mentioning what were some of the mistakes he made during his rule.

Listen carefully to the dialogue between the two officers, and then ask them: What pattern repeats itself in Saul's behavior? What happened when Saul became a jealous, destructive and bad-tempered person?

Ask the students to read the passage in 1 Samuel 28:3-24 in their Bible to reaffirm learning.

ACTIVITIES

What would have happened? What happened?

Divide the class into two groups to work on page 141 of the student worksheet. The first group will answer the questions in the first column, while those in group 2 will answer those in the second column. Make sure they have the correct answers before they write them in the blanks on the sheet.

What kind of behavior?

Ask your students the following questions, and write the answers on the board:

- What kind of pattern is forming in Nate's life?
- What can he do to change it?
- Now think about your own life. What kind of actions do you frequently carry out?
- Are you forming positive, beneficial patterns for your life?
- Do you show love, honor, service and obedience to God?

Give them time to write the answers in the triangles on page 142.

TO FINISH

We suggest that you set aside some time to guide your students to examine their own lives, seeing if there is something they should confess to God for having disobeyed His Word. Direct them in prayer, and before saying goodbye, review the Memory verse.

Can there be a good king?

Biblical References: 2 Samuel 11-12; Psalm 51.

Lesson Objective: That pre-teens learn to recognize and confess their faults to God.

Memory Verse: *And now, Israel, what does the Lord your God ask of you but to fear the Lord your God, to walk in obedience to him, to love him, to serve the Lord your God with all your heart and with all your soul* (Deuteronomy 10:12).

PREPARE YOURSELF TO TEACH!

Repentance and confession are essential for people to restore their relationship with God. Of course, it is not easy for anyone to admit their sin and turn away from it. It is easier to make excuses, blame others or try to cover up sin. When preteens do something wrong, they may try to do what Saul did. But, they must understand that they can not receive the forgiveness of sins unless they recognize it and turn away from it.

This lesson tells us about one of the great heroes of the Bible: David. Students will be able to compare how Saul and David acted in the face of sin, and how those attitudes made a difference in their relationship with God and their future. In the midst of a society in which sin is tolerated, and many times it is concealed, your students must recognize when they have sinned before God, confess it and repent from the heart.

BIBLICAL COMMENTARY

2 Samuel 11-12. The story of David is one of the best known in the Bible. It is very interesting to read how a humble shepherd became the most important king of Israel.

Although David performed many feats and his stories are impressive, we must not forget that he was also human. One time, he stayed in Jerusalem after sending Joab to battle and committed adultery with Bathsheba, the wife of Uriah. Upon learning that she was pregnant, David wanted to cover up his sin. Therefore, he tried to get Uriah to be with his wife in order to justify the future birth of the baby. When that did not work, he ordered Uriah to be put on the battle front to die.

God used the prophet Nathan to pronounce judgment against David. In similar circumstances, Saul would have given excuses and blamed others, but David admitted his sin and asked for forgiveness. Psalm 51 relates David's confession.

This king was a great political leader and military strategist who gave Israel important victories, stability and peace. The secret of his success was that he was willing to confess his sin, and he repented heartily, allowing God to continue guiding his life. Because of his devotion to God and his sincere confession, he is considered the most remarkable king of Israel.

DEVELOPMENT OF THE LESSON

Deuteronomy 10:12. Welcome your students, and have them sit in a circle to review the Memory verse. A volunteer should start by saying the first word of the verse. Then, the next in the circle will say the second, and so on until they complete the verse. Another option is that, also in a circle, pass from hand to hand a small ball to the beat of song, until the leader says "Stop!" Whoever has the ball must say the following part of the verse, and so on until everyone has participated.

Review

Ask your students if during the week they noticed in themselves or in a friend a pattern of constant disobedience. Then, ask them how they responded to the directions of their parents or teachers. If you wish, use the following questions:

- Did you do something this week that you would have preferred not to have done?
- What kind of pattern of behavior are you showing in your life?

Remind them that they can ask God for help when they are facing temptation and having trouble being obedient. Then tell them: In the stories of the previous classes, we learned that Saul was the first king of Israel. At the beginning of his reign he acted correctly; he was humble, obedient and willing to allow God to guide his life. Then, he became selfish, disobedient and proud. When he sinned, he did not sincerely repent, but tried to blame others for the wrong that he had committed. In today's story, we will study the king who succeeded Saul on the throne of Israel.

Simon says

Choose a student to be the leader. He should come forward and make gestures or actions while giving orders: Simon says to touch your nose. Everyone must follow the leader and perform the action. But if he gives the instruction without saying "Simon says" (for example: raise your left leg), the others should not obey.

To make it more fun, combine two actions (for example: Simon says raise your left leg and right arm). If anyone makes a mistake in following the instructions, he must sit down and wait for the game to end.

Then, talk to them and ask them:

- Was there any action you did not want to do?
- What happened when you did not follow the instructions?

Listen to their answers, and explain that this is just a game. However, in real life there are also consequences when we disobey, when we do not follow the instructions and break the rules. In today's story we will learn about a man who committed a grave sin and did not know what to do.

How do you rate them?

Have the students find worksheet page 143. They are to rate how Saul and David did in each area, based on the stories they have learned and what they know about the lives of David and Saul.

BIBLE STORY

Read 2 Samuel 11-12 in advance to become familiar with the Bible story and be prepared to explain it to your students.

Spend time in class reading chapter 11 of 2 Samuel. Read the text, making the appropriate intonation for this type of story, while the class follows the story, each in their own Bible.

It is likely that many questions will arise from the preteens about David's attitude. That is why it is important that you are ready to respond and help them understand that David made a mistake, but God forgave him, restored him and prospered him as king.

ACTIVITIES

Caught you!

The big difference between Saul and David was how each reacted after disobeying. On the worksheet page 144 is a list of six verses that will allow your students to compare the reactions of the two kings. Give them time to look up each verse and write down which character it is talking about.

- 1 Samuel 15:13-16 (Saul tried to cover his sin by blaming others.)
- 2 Samuel 11:14-15 (David tried to hide his sin with Bathsheba by killing the husband, General Uriah.)
- 1 Samuel 15:24-25 (Saul repented of his sin, but asked for the company of Samuel to keep up appearances.)
- 2 Samuel 12:5-7, 13 (David was angry with the story of the man who took the poor man's only sheep. When he realized that the prophet Nathan was referring to him, David confessed his sin.)
- Psalm 51:1-4 (David admitted his sin and asked for mercy from God.)
- 1 Samuel 15:30 (Saul said that he had sinned, but perhaps he was more interested in the opinion that people had about him than in repentance of heart.)

Oh no!

When David realized what he had done, he confessed his sin, asked for God's mercy, and wrote Psalm 51, a psalm of confession. Ask your class to read it and answer the following question: What does this psalm tell us about the type of person David was?

What does God ask of Christians?

Have the students go to page 146, and read the phrase in the center of the circle and the questions from the other sections. Have them look up the biblical passages and write the answers in the spaces.

TO FINISH

To conclude the class, remind the preteens of what Nathan the prophet told David: that although he had sinned in secret, everyone would know his sin. Maybe nobody else knows their wrong behaviors, but God is aware of everything we do.

Lead them in a prayer of confession and repentance, and encourage them to live according to God's will.

Lesson 40

The fall of a wise king

Biblical References: 1 Kings 3; 4:29-34; 9:1-9; 11:1-13.

Lesson Objective: That the preteens understand the importance of obeying God and remaining firm in their promises.

Memory Verse: *And now, Israel, what does the Lord your God ask of you but to fear the Lord your God, to walk in obedience to him, to love him, to serve the Lord your God with all your heart and with all your soul* (Deuteronomy 10:12).

PREPARE YOURSELF TO TEACH!

Have you ever heard your students belittle themselves? Do not be surprised. Physical changes, school challenges and growing concern about what peers think make preteens think badly about themselves. They may feel uncomfortable with the changes they are experiencing; or when compared to the beauty prototypes that the media preaches, they may ask themselves: "How can I be beautiful, strong or smart like them?"

This lesson will teach them that for God there is something more important than beauty, strength and knowledge: obedience out of love. Even being the wisest man in the world, King Solomon made bad decisions every time he disobeyed God. In Deuteronomy 10:12, we do not read that beauty, strength and knowledge were part of the requirements to develop a good relationship with God, but rather to honor, love, serve and obey Him.

BIBLICAL COMMENTARY

1 Kings 3; 4:29-34; 9:1-9; 11:1-13. Solomon was less than 20 years old when he became the new king of Israel. What a huge responsibility for a young man! He was to rule a great nation, taking the place of David, a man after God's own heart (1 Samuel 13:14).

The covenant that God had made with David was now the responsibility of Solomon. That is why he said to God: "I am young" (1 Kings 3:7), and asked him to give him an "understanding heart" (3:9).

God honored his request by giving him wisdom; in addition, He gave him wealth, honor and long life. The only condition was that he walk in the ways of God, keeping his precepts and commandments as David, his father (3:14) had done.

But Solomon did not fulfill his part of the covenant. From the beginnings of his reign he was inconsistent in his observance of the law. He married foreign women, practiced worship rituals in forbidden places and, as often happens, all this led to disobedience.

Deuteronomy 17:17 forbade the Israelite king from having many wives. Solomon broke that law by having 700 wives and 300 concubines. These foreign women alienated him from the one true God, bringing judgment against Solomon.

The 40 years of Solomon's reign ended in chaos and violence. Honoring the covenant with David, God allowed Rehoboam, David's grandson, to reign over Judah. The tribe of Benjamin joined Judah, while the other 10 tribes united under the rule of Jeroboam.

DEVELOPMENT OF THE LESSON

Wish box

For this activity you will need newspapers or magazines, scissors, glue, paper or letter-size cards and markers. Ask each student, using the magazines and newspapers, to make a collage type picture with everything they would like to have. When they finish, write the passage of Proverbs 3:13-15 in the same box.

Wise people

Ask the class to name people they consider wise. Write the names on the board and ask them: Why do you think they are wise? Are they really wise, or just have much knowledge? Is there a difference between wisdom and knowledge? Write the words "Knowledge" and "Wisdom" on the board, and have a dictionary on hand to find the meanings.

The wisdom of the world vs. the wisdom of God

Divide the class into two groups. Give each one three statements from page 147 of the worksheet. Allow them to debate whether each statement refers to the wisdom of God or the wisdom of the world.

Tell them that today's lesson will explain more about the difference between what people think and what God knows is best for us.

BIBLE STORY

To tell this story, study the following passages in advance: 1 Kings 9:4-7; Ecclesiastes 1:12-14; 1 Kings 11:11-13.

Before beginning the story, ask that they sit in a circle and look in their Bible for the study passages. As you tell the story, ask a student to read the passage you want to emphasize. In conclusion, explain that when Solomon died, his son Rehoboam reigned over the tribe of Judah, and the tribe of Benjamin joined it. Jeroboam became the king of the ten remaining tribes.

ACTIVITIES

Promises and warnings

Have them find worksheet page 148. There they will find a biblical passage that talks about what God promised Solomon, and the conditions necessary for it to be fulfilled. Tell your students to read the paragraph and circle the promise. Then underline the conditions, and with double lines the warning.

Consequences

Allow time for your students to read 1 Kings 11:11-13. Then, complete the verses found on page 149 of the worksheet. Then, discuss what could have happened if Solomon had kept the covenant he made with God and obeyed his commandments. Explain that the consequence of his disobedience was that the kingdom was divided and the people returned to sin, worshiping false idols.

What's wrong with me now?

Help your students reflect on the four requirements for maintaining a right relationship with God. Use the following questions to guide your group meditation time:

- What are the four requirements to maintain a good relationship with God?

- Which of these requirements is hardest to fulfill?

- What can you do this week to strengthen your relationship with God?

If they find it difficult to love God, encourage them to examine everything that may be interfering with them and their love for him.

On the other hand, if they can not obey God, help them think about the times they are obedient, so that when they are tempted to disobey, remember that God helps and strengthens them.

If they are struggling to honor God, motivate them to take time to think about His greatness.

Finally, if they have difficulty serving God, help them prepare a schedule that includes some type of service, or invite them to get involved in some church ministry.

TO FINISH

Use the questions on page 150 to review the unit. Then, thank God for the teachings received in this unit, and encourage them to follow the four steps to have a good relationship with God. After recognizing the effort of those who learned the Memory verse of the unit, sing some praise songs before saying goodbye. Remind them that next week they will begin the study of a new unit, entitled: "How to be happy."

HOW TO BE HAPPY

Biblical basis: Matthew 5:1-12, 43-48; 18:21-35; Luke 14:1, 7-14; 18:9-14; 23:26-43.

Memory verse of the unit: *Blessed are those who hunger and thirst for righteousness, for they will be filled.* (Matthew 5:6).

Purposes of the unit

This unit will help preteens to:

- Understand the teachings of Jesus about happiness.
- Examine their attitudes in light of the teachings of Jesus.
- Experience the happiness that comes from obeying the teachings of Jesus.

Lessons from the unit

Lesson 41: What is happiness?

Lesson 42: Happiness is ... obeying God

Lesson 43: Should I forgive?

Lesson 44: Victorious in Christ

Why do pre-teens need the teaching of this unit?

The search for happiness is a common goal of people. However, many, in trying to find it, go astray on the wrong paths.

On the other hand, the true meaning of happiness has been misunderstood, substituting it for riches, pleasure, well-being and power. According to the prevailing ideology in our society, happiness depends on money, social status, job success and interpersonal relationships. For all this, it is common for preadolescents to have egocentric attitudes, thinking that happiness is determined by popularity, purchasing power or clothes. However, the Bible offers us a completely different perspective.

Self-centeredness is not a new problem; it also reigned in the days of Jesus. At that time, people sought happiness in a frenetic way as is done today.

Jesus taught that we are happy if we have a good relationship with God and with our neighbor. Pre-teens should know that the secret to having true happiness is obedience, love, humility, righteousness, mercy and forgiveness.

Lesson 41
What is happiness?

Biblical References: Matthew 5:1-12; Luke 14:1,7-14.

Lesson Objective: That pre-teens understand that if they are humble and gentle, they will find happiness.

Memory Verse: *Blessed are those who hunger and thirst for righteousness, for they will be filled.* (Matthew 5:6).

PREPARE YOURSELF TO TEACH!

In our society, the meaning of happiness has been distorted in such a way that many people do not know it. For most, happiness is about getting what you want when you want it. Television and advertising have been responsible for spreading the idea that happiness is the result of satisfying all desires. For example, if young people do not have the latest fashionable clothes or the latest video game console or the latest cell phone, they feel that they are depriving them of something they should have, and therefore they are unhappy. That is, their state of mind is determined by purchasing power and popularity.

However, the Word of God teaches us that only in Jesus do we find complete happiness. That is what Jesus taught in the Sermon on the Mount and in other parables.

It is important that your students learn to examine themselves and differentiate between desire and need. They must know God's plan in order to survive in a society dominated by greed. Some may be trapped in the insatiable desire to have all that this world offers, but they should know that only in Jesus do we find the way to true happiness.

BIBLICAL COMMENTARY

Matthew 5:1-12. The Beatitudes, with which the Sermon on the Mount begins, constitute the first of the five sermons of Jesus that Matthew includes in his Gospel.

The word "blessed" (or happy) refers to the spiritual joy one feels when God approves of his conduct. Therefore, the Beatitudes describe the qualities and characteristics of the true disciple of Christ, showing that he can experience inner peace and joy, despite external circumstances.

"Poor in spirit" (Matthew 5:3) are those who, recognizing their spiritual need, understand that they must depend on God in everything. True humility results from recognizing that everything we are, or hope to be, comes from God.

The term "meek" (Matthew 5:5) is often misinterpreted, associating meekness with timidity or false humility. Meekness is not a form of weakness, but a spiritual condition in which we recognize that God is in control. The meek are those who have discipline to follow God's direction and accept what He allows.

Luke 14:1,7-14. In the parable of the wedding feast, Jesus gave a lesson to the guests who wished to occupy the positions of honor. Everyone knew that seats near the host were for special guests. Those who struggled to occupy the first places showed their pride and the concept they had about themselves. However, those seats were reserved for people whom the host considered special.

The teaching of the parable is that God does not like us to honor ourselves. Rather, let others honor us. This point of view is contrary to that of the world, where each person defends his own interests first.

DEVELOPMENT OF THE LESSON

You learned?

Take a moment to talk about what happened during the week: classes, homework, vacations, football matches, etc.

After reviewing what they learned last week about Solomon's life, ask them: What positive teachings do we find in the life of Solomon? Emphasize the importance of obeying God and his Word. Maybe some pre-teens are attending a Christian education class for the first time, and they do not want to talk about their experiences because it's something new for them.

Little by little, your students will assume greater responsibility for what they do or do not do every day of the week. This must occur naturally, not under pressure or out of fear.

What makes you happy?

Ask that everyone writes everything that makes them feel happy on the board or on a large paper sheet. Then, decide together how to number them according to their importance.

Then ask them:

- How long do you think this will make you happy?

- Can any of the above be destroyed easily?

- If what we wrote down disappeared, how do you think it would affect the lives of those your age?

Explain that many times, people seek happiness in the wrong people or places, and their mood changes according to the possessions they have or what happens to them each day. That means that their mood is temporary and that its foundation is not safe.

Tell them: In today's class we will learn the secret to enjoy happiness in a genuine and true way.

BIBLE STORY

The beatitudes

Write the word "BEATITUDE" on the board or on a card. Ask the class if they know the meaning of that word. Listen to their responses, and explain that "beatitude" means happiness, blessing and approval from God. The blessed person is a happy person. But it is not the kind of happiness that the world offers, but one that is enduring and eternal.

Read together Luke 14:1,7-14. Then, have your students explain what they understood from the passage. Supplement the information in light of the Word of God.

ACTIVITIES

Look closer!

Hand out the student worksheet p 152. Divide the class into small groups to answer the questions about Luke 14:7-11. When they have finished, share answers and review the Bible passage.

Create a story!

Allow time for your class to work on p. 153 of the worksheet. They should write in the blanks what they think happens in each scene. Talk about the attitude that Christians should have when they suffer injustices and are mistreated. Ask some volunteers to tell what they wrote.

My commitment

Guide your students to silently read each of the pledges on page 154, and mark the ones they promise to follow. This activity should be personal, helping them reflect on the importance of committing to God to change their attitude.

If you can, prepare cards with these promises. Distribute them so that each student can carry one with them to remember their commitment to God during the week.

TO FINISH

Gather them together to pray and give thanks to God for teaching all of you through the Beatitudes the secret of happiness. Intercede for the sick, and encourage everyone to attend the next class. Do not forget to call or visit those who were absent.

Happiness is ... obeying God

Biblical References: Matthew 5:6; Luke 18:9-14.

Lesson Objective: That the students discover the joy of having a good relationship with God.

Memory Verse: *Blessed are those who hunger and thirst for righteousness, for they will be filled.* (Matthew 5:6).

PREPARE YOURSELF TO TEACH!

A Christian author wrote a song which he called, "Social party," in which he describes the class of young people in Sunday School as simply a social party. This song does not apply to all Sunday School classes of pre-teens and young people, but the unfortunate thing is that it describes some of them very well.

It is important to mention that young people have the necessary maturity to seriously examine their relationship with God. Although they must still mature in many areas of their lives, they have the ability to decide whether their commitment to God is real or whether they will only follow a religion. However, we know that what God wants is a total commitment.

Through this lesson, your students will understand that God wants to help them build their relationship with Him, no matter how adverse the circumstances may be. They will also understand what Jesus wants to teach us through the Beatitudes, and what it means to be hungry and thirsty for justice.

BIBLICAL COMMENTARY

Matthew 5:6. Hunger and thirst for righteousness are spiritual needs. God wants us to seek righteousness, and this is an essential element of our life. Often, we do not consider it as such, but in fact it is. When we want to love and honor God, and follow his ways, we are on the right path to hunger and thirst for righteousness.

Luke 18:9-14. This passage shows the difference between internal righteousness and external hypocrisy and piety. What looks good on the outside may be hiding the rotten inside. The Pharisee's prayer was actually a list of his good works, while that of the publican, who begged for mercy, showed his need for God.

The publican was hungry and thirsty for righteousness. Instead, the Pharisee was satisfied with a false righteousness centered on himself.

DEVELOPMENT OF THE LESSON

Anonymous letters

For this activity you will need magazines, glue, scissors and paper.

Ask your students if they have ever sent an anonymous letter so the receiver would not recognize them. Explain that the characteristic of these letters is that they do not bear a signature, so it is difficult to recognize the author.

Tell them that in this activity, they should write an anonymous letter to one of their classmates. To write the letter, they must cut out letters or words from magazines, and put together the Bible verse found in Matthew 5:6. Each student will make his own letter. Then, anonymously, they will give it to a classmate.

Each student must take home the letter they received to review the Memory verse. Then, they must bring it with them to the next class.

A mirage

Hand out the student worksheets, and have them find page 155 and observe the illustration carefully, while a volunteer reads the definition of "mirage" aloud. Then, reflect and answer the questions at the bottom of the page.

Explain that although many of us have not experienced what it means to "faint from hunger or thirst," we can imagine the despair of a person lost in the middle of the hot desert, with the desire to drink something that refreshes them.

In the same way, people seek happiness, and sometimes resort to incorrect methods to try to achieve it. In today's class we will learn what Jesus said about this.

Congratulations...

Ask students to look at page 156, and work in pairs or small groups. They should list ten different ways through which people seek happiness (for example: success, popularity, cars, money, position, friends, possessions, fame, etc.).

Then, ask some volunteers to read what they wrote. Write down the most common answers on the board. Tell them that in today's Bible story they will learn what Jesus taught about happiness.

BIBLE STORY

Ask your students to look up Luke 18:9-14 and read it in silence. Then, explain that during his earthly ministry, Jesus traveled through many places and met the physical and material needs of the people. That is why he dedicated a large part of his time to healing the sick and caring for the needy. Jesus also observed the attitude of the people. For example, some were humble and avoided pride; others trusted in their own righteousness and were proud. For that reason, Jesus related the parable of the publican and the Pharisee.

Encourage a time of reflection on the biblical passage and the way it should be applied to the lives of preadolescents.

ACTIVITIES

What is the difference?

Ask your students: What is the difference between the Pharisee's prayer and the publican's prayer? Allow some to respond.

Next, explain that the difference had to do with their focus. The Pharisee focused his prayer on his good deeds and on the high view he had of himself. However, the publican asked for mercy, recognizing his unworthiness before God. For that reason, God heard and answered the sincere prayer of the publican.

According to what we have learned today, which of the two men was hungry and thirsty for righteousness?

What is righteousness?

Have them turn to page 157 and read the definitions of righteous and righteousness. Give them time to talk about what they understood, and help them understand the concepts they have doubts about. Have them write Matthew 5:6 in their own words. Then, turn the page to answer the questions.

TO FINISH

Have your students sit in a circle and tell them: Through the Beatitudes, Jesus teaches us that blessed people are those who recognize their true spiritual condition and strive to know God and his righteousness. That is as important as water and food in the desert. We are to be thirsty and hungry for the righteousness of God. Do you think that having a good relationship with God is as important as eating or drinking? Give a few minutes to reflect, and ask: What do you need to change in your life to be hungry and thirsty for righteousness?

According to the answers, encourage them to seek God with humility and fervor, study the Word and continue attending church. Repeat the Memory verse once more.

Ask the students to answer the questions on page 158 to review the lesson.

Then, intercede for them and invite them to the next class.

Should I forgive?

Biblical References: Matthew 5:7; 18:21-35.

Lesson Objective: That the pre-adolescents learn that happiness is found through forgiveness and mercy.

Memory Verse: *Blessed are those who hunger and thirst for righteousness, for they will be filled (Matthew 5:6).*

PREPARE YOURSELF TO TEACH!

When people hurt us, our natural reaction is to get revenge. Resentment and bitterness are nested in the heart, generating serious emotional and spiritual problems.

I meet parents who, on the pretext of helping their children mature and be respected, teach them how to fight and defend themselves. However, in the Sermon on the Mount, Jesus taught something completely different.

Forgiveness and mercy are two concepts that are difficult to understand for most people, but for those of us who walk in the light of Christ, they must be goals to follow.

Pre-teens must learn to forgive those who hurt them. Perhaps many of them receive insults, even abuse, and do not understand why they should forgive the one who hurts them. Jesus' teaching on how to show mercy is a very different concept from what pre-teens see around them. But they must understand that only through the grace of God can we be merciful.

BIBLICAL COMMENTARY

Matthew 5:7; 18:21-35. It is important to understand that mercy is not synonymous with pity. Pity is the emotional response to a situation that causes sadness, but that does not prompt action. Mercy includes not only recognizing the need, but accepting the responsibility to do something without expecting reward. Mercy is active, not passive. Even when we do not deserve mercy, God gives it to us without needing to do something in return.

In antiquity, the Romans did not practice mercy, because they believed that each one should receive what he deserved. They abhorred every sign of pity, compassion and weakness, considering that the merciful were weak. The Pharisees also had no mercy on the one who violated the rules, stating that suffering was the just punishment for sins. Therefore, Jesus' call to be merciful was revolutionary and challenging.

In the parable of this lesson, the king had mercy on his servant and forgave him a debt that was so big that the servant had no way of paying for it. However, the servant did not want to forgive his fellow servant an insignificant debt.

The servant represents the selfish person who always expects to receive consideration and special treatment, but refuses to treat others like that.

Jesus wanted to teach Peter, and us today, this lesson: The children of God must forgive and be merciful without expecting anything in return.

DEVELOPMENT OF THE LESSON

Anonymous letters

After welcoming your students, and singing some songs of praise, we suggest that you start the lesson by reviewing the Memory verse. For that you will need the letters that they prepared the previous class.

Ask each student to paste their letter on the board, while repeating the Memory verse. When all the letters are attached, repeat the verse together. Try to guess who each of them belongs to, and allow each one to take their work home.

Here comes the judge!

Try to set up the class room as if it were a courtroom. Have a judge's chair, a place for the accused and the public. For this dialogue you will need the participation of four volunteers: one will play the judge and the other three will represent the accused; the rest will be the public. If possible, provide a wooden hammer for the judge. The judge must enter the room and sit behind the table. Defendants should read the following statements.

Defendant 1: Your Honor, this is my first crime. I stole from a store and I'm very sorry. I beg you to have mercy on me!

Defendant 2: Your Honor, this is my third crime. The police captured me in an armed assault, but I do not deserve to be here. The police would not have caught me if it had not been for my partner's clumsiness. Please have mercy on me this time!

Defendant 3: Your Honor, I've been here 14 times. It seems that someone wants me to appear guilty again and again. They caught me in an assault with a firearm, but the laws of this country are unfair. I am a nice person, educated, and I promise that I will not do it again. Please have mercy on me.

Allow the judge to decide each case, and then allow time for others to express their opinions about the verdicts.

Should I forgive?

Ask students to find page 159. Instruct them to work in pairs to reflect on what is happening in the illustration, and answer the four questions.

Then, ask that a volunteer look up Matthew 5:1-12 and read it out loud. Tell them: The blessedness that we will study today tells us that we are blessed (we receive the approval of God, and the peace and happiness that comes with it) when we are merciful and forgive the people who have wronged us.

BIBLE STORY

Read the study passage (Matthew 18:15-35) in advance, and give it to your students in your own words. Another option is to read the passage to the class using a paraphrase of the Bible to make it easier to understand. Allow time for them to ask questions or express their doubts, and respond in light of the Word of God.

What does the Bible say about forgiveness?

Have your students work on page 160, filling in the spaces to complete the biblical verses. Next, ask four volunteers to read them out loud. Verify that everyone has written the correct words.

Ideas for the teacher

Maybe pre-teens get tired or bored of having the room set up the same week after week. Try to vary according to the teaching method you will use.

If you will have a group discussion, arrange the chairs in a circle. If you will divide the class into small groups, and conditions permit, form several circles of a few chairs in different parts of the room. If you plan any activity or game, push the chairs towards the walls, to leave an empty space in the center of the room.

If necessary, change the location of the chairs once or twice during the class. In any case, always ask for the help of your students. Pre-teens enjoy that little break in the middle of the lesson.

TO FINISH

Allow time for everyone to put the room in order before saying goodbye.

Choose a volunteer to lead in a closing prayer, asking the Lord to help you all forgive and be merciful to one another.

Encourage them to practice the Bible teachings during the week. Remind them that the next class will be the last on the Beatitudes, and that it is very important that no one misses the class.

Victorious in Christ

Biblical References: Matthew 5:10-12, 43-48; Luke 23:26-43.

Lesson Objective: That the preadolescents find consolation in the promises of God if they are persecuted for their faith.

Memory Verse: *Blessed are those who hunger and thirst for righteousness, for they will be filled.* (Matthew 5:6).

PREPARE YOURSELF TO TEACH!

Religious persecution is a painful truth of our day, although people try to cover it under the curtain of tolerance and respect for human rights. With surprise we can say that those who most demand tolerance are those who tolerate Christians the least. It is common for the media to ridicule or unfavorably represent believers. Although preadolescents may not identify with physical persecution, they must know other forms of persecution that Christians face today.

The Bible tells us about it. The story of the crucifixion of Christ is the ultimate example of persecution. Jesus, who never sinned, suffered persecution until death, giving us the example of how to face it.

This lesson also tells us about the promises that God gives in the Beatitudes to those who suffer persecution for their faith. Pre-teens will learn that God will be with them every time they face persecution.

BIBLICAL COMMENTARY

Matthew 5:10-12, 43-48. What Jesus taught in the Sermon on the Mount about persecution is fascinating. He stated that many Christians would be persecuted for their beliefs, and that others had suffered previously because of their faith. Then, he taught what is the proper attitude when suffering persecution: be glad and rejoice (5:12), love your enemies and pray for those who persecute you (5:44).

Luke 23:26-43. Jesus endorsed his words about persecution by giving the supreme example. Although he was innocent, he experienced physical and mental anguish before his crucifixion. He suffered derision, torture and other cruel mistreatments. He faced the hypocrisy of those who had praised him before but now were screaming for him to be crucified.

In Luke 23:34, we read Jesus' answer: "Father, forgive them, because they do not know what they are doing." Jesus practiced what he preached. That is why he prayed for those who sent him to a cross of pain, persecution and death. How much do we need to experience the deep relationship that Jesus had with his Father!

DEVELOPMENT OF THE LESSON

Heroes

Show a trophy, or a photo of a person receiving a trophy or medal. Ask your students to mention someone who deserves the title of hero because he/she overcame a very difficult situation. Explain that those who receive the title of "hero" are those who managed to overcome obstacles through perseverance and strength, becoming stronger people having gone through those situations. Give them time to find worksheet page 161 and write the name of someone they consider a hero and why.

Search the concordance

To carry out this activity, it is necessary to have a Bible with a concordance. Ask them to look for the word "blessed", and count how many verses in which this word is mentioned. Next, ask them to look for the word "blessing", and also to count the times it is mentioned.

BIBLE STORY

Have your students sit down forming a circle. Then ask them to recount an incident in which their friends made fun of them for doing the right thing and not following others. Use the answers to introduce the topic of study. Tell them that today they will talk about how Christians can face persecution.

Beatitudes

Divide the class into two teams. Give each group a card or paper. Tell them they have 5 minutes to read and write the following verses in their own words: Matthew 5:10-12 and Matthew 5:43-48.

Then, come together to listen to the conclusions of each team.

At the end of the activities, tell the biblical story referred to in Luke 22 and 23.

What does the Bible tell us?

Have students go to page 162 and cross out the boxes that have a triangle in the corner. That way they will find the hidden phrases.

Explain that as human beings, it is difficult for us to imagine how we would react to persecution, but God gives his children the grace and help they need at the right time.

Now divide the class into three groups to read the cases or examples on page 163. As a teacher, you will need to become familiar with these examples and then guide the preteens in a discussion that everyone participates in. In each case, a question is repeated: "What are you doing?" Allow everyone to give their opinion.

Then, give them time to complete the unit's last project, found on page 164, by making a poster based on the words of Matthew 5:10-12.

TO FINISH

Being persecuted is not something pleasant. It may seem impossible to "rejoice and be happy," as Jesus taught. However, God tells us that if we face persecution, we can express our concern and fear; we can also pray to try to stop it, just as Jesus did in the Garden of Gethsemane. In addition, we must pray for strength to face the persecution.

Encourage the preteens to have the freedom to express if they feel they are being persecuted because they are Christians. Maybe in the family of one of them, the father or the mother does not have the same faith and that creates conflicts. Pray for them that during the week they will have strength and confidence in God's protection.

Also, intercede for the brothers and sisters who suffer persecution around the world, mainly in Indonesia, China, India, Pakistan, North Korea, Sudan, Egypt and Vietnam. Commit yourself to pray every day for the Christians of a country, asking God to protect them and give them the courage to overcome suffering.

Remind them that the true secret of happiness is in obeying the teachings of Jesus and living according to the will of God.

notes

THE COURAGE OF DANIEL

Biblical basis: Daniel 1-3; 5-6; Hebrews 11:32-12:3.

Unit Verse: *Therefore, since we are surrounded by such a great cloud of witnesses, let us throw off everything that hinders and the sin that so easily entangles. And let us run with perseverance the race marked out for us* (Hebrews 12:1).

Purposes of the unit

This unit will help preteens to:

• Understand that Christians face external pressures that will try to change their way of thinking.

• Know that faith in God is the basis for being brave.

• Commit to honor God regardless of the consequences.

• Seek the help of God when they face persecution because of their faith.

Lessons of the unit

Lesson 45: Defend your beliefs

Lesson 46: Trust in the wisdom of God

Lesson 47: Have the courage to be honest

Lesson 48: Have the courage to stand firm

Why do pre-teens need the teaching of this unit?

At this stage of their development, preadolescents face serious identity problems and want others to accept them. It is common for them to worry about what others think of them and try to do anything to identify with the group. For that reason, sometimes they easily give in to pressure and conform to what the world offers them.

Most Christian preteens want to please God, but they require adult support to make decisions that honor the Lord. They need to have positive role models nearby to help them live as God wants, encouraging them to defend their faith and resist the temptation to act like others. The life and testimony of Daniel, Azariah, Mishael and Ananias (Shadrach, Meshach, and Abednego) will be an excellent example for your students. Help them understand that, although they were young and living in a terrible situation, they obeyed God and defended their faith.

Lesson 45
Defend your beliefs

Biblical Reference: Daniel 1.

Lesson Objective: That students will decide to defend their faith in God, despite difficult situations.

Memory Verse: *Therefore, since we are surrounded by such a great cloud of witnesses, let us throw off everything that hinders and the sin that so easily entangles. And let us run with perseverance the race marked out for us* (Hebrews 12:1).

PREPARE YOURSELF TO TEACH!

As your students grow up, they face greater pressure from their friends to participate in inappropriate activities. Therefore, they need to know how to face the pressure and defend their beliefs.

Since they still do not fully understand the results of their actions, they do not take into account that their decisions will affect their relationship with God and their Christian witness. Through these lessons, help them understand the difference between Christian values and those of the world, and what it means to live correctly in the midst of a world full of sin.

This lesson will motivate them to stand firm in their faith in God, even if that does not make them popular and, in some cases, is risky. Explain to your students that Daniel and his three friends were teenagers when they went through this experience. This will help them to identify with them, and to understand how important it is to remain steadfast in the Christian life.

BIBLICAL COMMENTARY

Daniel 1. Jehoiakim, king of Judah, was an evil man who led his people to the worship of idols. Because of that sin, God allowed Nebuchadnezzar, king of Babylon, to conquer them and take thousands of Jews captive.

Daniel and his three friends were taken to Babylon around 605 B.C. Then there was a second deportation, in 597 B.C. And the last one was in 586 B.C., when the Babylonians destroyed the temple and the holy city.

Nebuchadnezzar sought among the exiles people who held important positions in the defeated kingdom. He needed men to administer matters related to the Jews. The chief of the eunuchs chose Daniel and his friends Ananias, Mishael and Azariah to receive special training.

The four young people were intelligent, healthy and good looking. It was the custom of the king to choose young people or teenagers to indoctrinate them and teach them the Babylonian customs.

That process included changing the names of Daniel and his friends. Their Jewish names reminded them of their faith in God; nevertheless, the new Babylonian names honored false gods. Daniel (God is my judge) became Belteshazzar (may Baal protect my life); Ananias (God shows grace) was transformed into Shadrach (Aku's command); Misael (who like God?) Became Meshach (who like Aku?); Azariah (God helps me) was transformed into Abednego (servant of Nego or Nebo).

The Mosaic Law forbade the Hebrews from eating unclean meat or food offered to idols. Daniel refused to follow the Babylonian customs that violated that law, and requested a different diet that did not compromise his convictions.

Daniel and his friends spoke with the chief of the eunuchs in a humble and friendly manner, and he agreed. God honored the courage and faithfulness of these young Hebrews, and blessed them by giving them better health, and greater knowledge and wisdom.

DEVELOPMENT OF THE LESSON

What does it mean?

During the week, find out the meaning of your name and that of your students.

Begin by explaining the meaning of your name. Then, ask them if they know the meaning of their respective names. Ask:

- Do you know why your parents gave you the name you have?
- If you could change it, what would you like to call yourself?

Give a little card to write the name they would like, and pin it to their shirt as an identification. During class, call them by the name they chose.

As the class progresses, ask how they feel when they hear you call them by a different name. Then tell them that today's class is about some young people whose names were changed.

Persecution

For this activity you will need a world map and colored pencils. Ask your students to locate: China, Pakistan, Iran, Afghanistan, Eritrea, Somalia, Laos, Vietnam, Malaysia, Sudan, Egypt, Libya, Algeria, Nigeria, India, Saudi Arabia, and North Korea. Instruct them to color each country with a different color. While doing so, explain that in those countries Christians are persecuted because of their faith. Search Christian magazines or the Internet for stories about this topic to tell your students.

Hang up the map in a visible place, and urge your class to commit themselves to pray daily for the persecuted brothers and sisters.

No, never ever!

Ask your students: Do you think there is something a Christian should never do? Listen to their answers.

Then distribute the student worksheets and ask them to find page 165 and write their answer in the rectangle at the top.

Next, instruct them to respond to the statements below using one of three alternatives: most, some, none. When finished, they should score 10 points for each time they marked the answer "none". Ask them to mention their total score. Maybe the scores are not that high, but it will help them understand how often we adapt to what others do.

Talk about what it means to conform, and ask them in what area they think young Christians have more problems: With money? The pressure of friends? Any secret? The style of clothes? Music?

In today's story, Daniel and his friends faced a difficult situation when the king's officers pressed them to do something that went against their beliefs.

Should I eat it?

A couple of weeks in advance, ask that some families bring food to share in class, or get cookies of different shapes and flavors.

Put the food on the table, and invite your students to choose the ones they want. While they are eating, ask them why they chose that particular food. Talk about your favorite foods, and ask them:

- Is there any food that their parents or dentist told them to avoid?
- Do you think it is a sin to eat any food?

After listening to their answers, conclude by telling them that although there are healthier foods than others, there are no laws that prohibit us from eating foods without nutritional value. In the Old Testament times, God commanded his people not to eat certain foods. In Leviticus 11, we find some of those prohibitions that God established, because the Israelites were surrounded by the Canaanites. For example, he forbade them from eating baby goat meat, because the Canaanites prepared that meat to offer it to their idols. God did not want his people to relate to idolatrous cults.

In today's story we will learn what some young Hebrews did when the king of Babylon commanded them to eat those forbidden foods.

BIBLE STORY

Ask your students to find Daniel 1 in their Bibles and have each one read a verse until the chapter ends. Or if you prefer, tell Daniel's story in your own words. Use this short introduction to start the story:

A long time ago, the people of God decided to disobey God's commandments and worship the pagan idols of neighboring peoples. As punishment, God allowed an enemy army to invade them.

Listen carefully to what I am going to tell you, so that you know what happened to a brave young man and three of his friends.

Continue with the story of Daniel chapter 1. When telling the story, make sure your students do not think that Daniel and his friends were vegetarians. Meat was not the problem. Some scholars affirm that the evil was that the meat had been dedicated to the idols. Others consider that participating in the meal represented an act of committed companionship. That is, by accepting the food of the king of Babylon, the young people would have made a commitment to him.

ACTIVITIES

Did Daniel conform?

Direct your students' attention to their worksheets, and give them time to read Daniel 1 and answer the five questions on page 166. They can work in groups or individually. When finished, ask them to read their answers.

Courage in the face of pressure

Ask them to look up Daniel 1:8 and ask: What is the third word of this verse? (resolved)

"Resolve" means to commit to perform a certain action. Daniel and his friends resolved in their hearts, or decided, not to break their beliefs. God honored their courage and firmness. The Bible says that He gave them wisdom, knowledge and understanding. Daniel had a plan. Let's see what it was:

- He resolved not to conform. He knew that the food and wine were bad for him and he did not give up, even though the head of the eunuchs at first rejected his request.

- He prepared a plan. God helped him draw up a plan that would allow him to continue on the right path. Remember how Daniel presented his request to the head of the officers.

- He trusted in God. In this case, God provided human help. The guard was willing to take a risk and give them 10 days of testing.

Then ask your students: What do you think you should do when you are tempted to act like everyone else?

- Decide that we will not commit to what is wrong.

- Think of an action plan to face temptation.

- Trust that God will help us.

How do we face temptation?

Write on the board or on a large sheet a list of areas in which preteens face peer pressure to be accepted: smoking, drinking alcoholic beverages, watching violent or sex videos, engaging in gossip or inappropriate comments, rude vocabulary, pornography, etc. Ask them to think about which of these areas they feel weakest, clarifying that they do not need to answer out loud. This activity must be very personal, and it is important that you give them time to reflect. Remind them that God is always willing to help them resist temptation and stand firm in their faith.

TO FINISH

Form a circle and lead them in prayer. Ask the Lord to give them courage and wisdom to overcome temptations and love the people who mistreat them because of their faith. Intercede for the Christians of the countries that were colored on the map.

Encourage them to attend the next class to continue learning about Daniel.

Lesson 46

Trust in the wisdom of God

Biblical References: Daniel 2.

Lesson Objective: That the pre-teens learn to trust God's wisdom.

Memory Verse: *Therefore, since we are surrounded by such a great cloud of witnesses, let us throw off everything that hinders and the sin that so easily entangles. And let us run with perseverance the race marked out for us* (Hebrews 12:1).

PREPARE YOURSELF TO TEACH!

As a normal part of their development, your students oscillate between the safety of childhood and the emotions of preadolescence and therefore, feel insecure. They seek to identify with their friends and have a place in the group. Since it is difficult for them to think about the consequences of their decisions, it seems easier to be guided by the group and behave like others to gain popularity.

As they grow in their knowledge of God, they will understand that he loves them and that divine wisdom can help them when faced with difficult situations. Divine wisdom is available to those who seek it.

In today's story, they will learn that although Daniel's life was in danger, he trusted in the wisdom of God.

In these times, preadolescents also face physical threats (for example, in gangs or when there is violence in the home). Others go through situations that threaten their psychological health. For this reason, it is important that through these biblical stories they learn to trust in divine wisdom to face adverse situations.

BIBLICAL COMMENTARY

Daniel 2. Nebuchadnezzar was the king of an important empire. One night, when he went to sleep, God spoke to him through a dream that left him worried and uneasy.

The king asked his whole court for help to know the meaning of that disturbing dream. However, he did not want to describe it. Perhaps he had forgotten the details when he woke up (v. 5), but it is also possible that he did not trust the wisdom of his servants (v. 9).

The wise men of the kingdom recognized that the task was impossible and that only a god could perform such a feat. This set the stage for God to manifest Himself through Daniel.

Faced with the inefficiency of those men, the king reacted with irrationality and ordered the death of all the wise men of the kingdom. In the middle of the crisis, Daniel requested more time to decipher the meaning of the dream. Daniel and his friends trusted that God, in his infinite wisdom, could help them, and so it was.

The dream was a description of world history that would develop from that moment forward. God used the image of an idol to reveal the future to them. And as Nebuchadnezzar worshiped idols, he could understand the symbolism. That figure represented the deterioration of the kingdoms. Many biblical scholars identify them as Babylon, Persia, Greece, and Rome. The quality and position of the metals were inferior in each kingdom. Finally, a stone not cut by man's hand, but by God, would destroy the other kingdoms. Christians affirm that this stone is Christ, and the mountain is the eternal kingdom of God.

Nebuchadnezzar, after understanding and recognizing the greatness of God, gave Daniel and his friends important positions within the kingdom.

DEVELOPMENT OF THE LESSON

Who do you trust in?

Discuss with the group the meaning of the word "trust". Then, ask them if there is a person to whom they would tell a very special secret. Then ask your students to look at worksheet page 167. There they will find a list of situations experienced by pre-teens in general. Students should write the name of a person they trust when they need help in each situation.

When the activity is over, tell them that in today's story they will learn what Daniel did when his life was in danger.

BIBLE STORY

Tell the Bible story in your own words, or with the participation of your students. Ask three volunteers to read Daniel 2:1-26.

You will be the narrator, one volunteer will read the part corresponding to Nebuchadnezzar, another will read what the Chaldean astrologers said and the last one will represent Daniel.

When you finish reading these verses, continue with the biblical account. If possible, get five objects or figures to illustrate the king's dream. As you mention the meaning of the dream, show the class the object that represents the part of the body that is mentioned.

Daniel told the king that in his dream he had seen the image of a man. The head was gold (show the gold object); the chest and arms, silver (show the silver object); the belly and the thighs, of bronze (show the bronze object); the legs were made of iron (show the iron object); and the feet, part iron and part clay (show the clay object).

ACTIVITIES

Did he understand the vision of Nebuchadnezzar?

Have the students keep their Bibles open to the study passage. Divide the class into pairs and give them time to answer the questions on page 168:

1. Why did the astrologers fail to explain the meaning of Nebuchadnezzar's dream? (Daniel 2:47)
2. What would happen to Daniel if he did not interpret the dream? (vv 12-13)
3. How did Daniel know the meaning? (vv 17-19)

4. Briefly describe the dream and its meaning (verses 29-45)
5. How did Daniel explain his ability to interpret the dream? (verses 27-28, 45).
6. What did Nebuchadnezzar learn about God?

Where can you find wisdom?

For this activity, preadolescents need to use the concordance found on page 169 of their worksheets. If you wish, continue working in pairs to help each other. The purpose is to use the concordance to decide which is the correct reference. They should write the reference inside the parentheses; then look in their Bible for the biblical verses to be sure they correspond to the reference.

What kind of wisdom does God give us?

Go to page 170. Have your students read the statements and cross out what they think God would not give us:

1. A guide to help you decide the right thing.
2. The answers to the exams when you did not study.
3. The ability to know the numbers so that you win the lottery.
4. A guide so you know when to invite someone to church.
5. Tips on how to get revenge when someone hurts you.
6. Tips on how to forgive someone who's hurt you.

Then, talk about the similarities between the crossed out sentences and the remaining sentences.

TO FINISH

Conclude the lesson asking: Do you ask God to give you wisdom before deciding something very important?

Guide your students to reflect on that topic. Then, pray giving thanks to God for the blessing of having His help and wisdom in the moments when we need them. Say goodbye by repeating the Memory verse.

Lesson 47

Have the courage to be honest

Biblical References: Daniel 5.

Lesson Objective: That the preteens understand what the judgment of God means.

Memory Verse: *Therefore, since we are surrounded by such a great cloud of witnesses, let us throw off everything that hinders and the sin that so easily entangles. And let us run with perseverance the race marked out for us* (Hebrews 12:1).

PREPARE YOURSELF TO TEACH!

Pre-teens often do not recognize the danger of disobeying until they suffer the consequences. Many people have the belief that "if they do not catch you, you are not in trouble." However, that way of thinking is dangerous, especially when they do not understand that their behavior harms others. Perhaps they justify their way of behaving by claiming that everyone does it. But preadolescents must know that God is holy and that one day he will judge everyone. The story of Belshazzar will show them that God's judgment is true.

As we said before, perhaps your students would be willing to compromise their beliefs to establish or maintain a friendship if the person acts or speaks contrary to Christian morals and beliefs. It is difficult for pre-teens to tell their classmates that they are doing something wrong. It is therefore important to teach them that, in the love of Christ, they have the obligation to warn or point out to their friends when they break the commandments of God.

BIBLICAL COMMENTARY

Daniel 5. When Daniel interpreted the dream of Nebuchadnezzar, he announced that the Medes and the Persians would defeat Babylon. Years later, when Belshazzar was the new king, he decided to hold a large banquet to which he invited his wives and concubines, which was forbidden. He also ordered his guards to bring him the sacred vessels of the temple of Jehovah that Nebuchadnezzar had stolen from Israel.

The king used these vessels to toast the pagan gods of Babylon. Perhaps he wanted to show that he was more powerful than Jehovah, the God who had announced the destruction of the empire.

Suddenly, the party was interrupted when a hand, without the rest of the body, began to write on the wall. The terrified king ordered his sages to interpret the writing, but they could not. Then the queen, remembering what Daniel had done in the past, recommended that they call him.

Daniel spoke fearlessly to the evil king, reminding him that Nebuchadnezzar had ignored God. In addition, he accused Belshazzar of deliberately rejecting God.

The words on the wall, written in Aramaic, accused Belshazzar of his sin. The message read: "counted, weighed and divided."

God had counted the days of Belshazzar, which had come to an end. God had weighed him in the balance and found him lacking. The Medes and the Persians would conquer the kingdom and divide it. God had dictated his judgment and, once again, confirmed his power.

DEVELOPMENT OF THE LESSON

Should I say it?

Gather and ask your students:

- Did you ever have to confront a friend or acquaintance of yours because they did something that was wrong?

- How do your friends feel when they have to confront others for doing something they should not do?

- Are they comfortable or afraid to tell the truth?

- Are there advantages or disadvantages when we confront others with the truth?

In today's story we will learn how Daniel confronted a king with a serious warning from God, and the king's reaction.

I don't want to hear it!

Distribute the student worksheets and ask to go to page 171.

Tell them: Not everyone likes to be told they are doing something wrong. Let's look at some sayings that preadolescents use when their friends confront them with the truth.

Give them time to read the expressions in the worksheet and, if they wish, supplement the information with their own contributions. Then, tell them that in today's story, Daniel had to confront someone with the truth of God.

BIBLE STORY

Today's story is about an inscription that appeared on a wall when a party was being held, and the king called Daniel to solve the mystery.

Write the words of the inscription on the board or on a card.

Ask the students to look up Daniel 5 and read it silently. Then, tell everyone the Bible story.

ACTIVITIES

A message

On page 173 of the student's book, they will find a board to write down some of the messages God has for preteens today. Use as references: Philippians 2:3; Colossians 3:2; Ephesians 6:1-3; Titus 3:1-2; and Deuteronomy 10:12.

As they work, tell them: God had a message for Belshazzar, and he let him know by writing it on the wall of the palace. Today God also has messages for us. However, He does not need to write them on the wall. They are written in the Bible, so that we can all read and understand them.

How can we tell the truth with love?

Allow time for your class to evaluate their attitude, according to the activity suggested on page 174 of the student worksheet:

- Are you talking about God's judgment (or yours)?

- Do you feel happy when you judge?

- When making a judgment, do you say it with love and to help?

- Can you respond with Christian love even if others do not understand your intentions?

Based on their answers, guide them to reflect on how we should speak to others about God's warnings. Then, encourage them to seek the direction of the Holy Spirit to address others with love and wisdom.

TO FINISH

This is a good time to lead your students in a time of prayer, thanking God for their blessings, and asking for strength to be able to tell others the truth.

Give them time to review the memory verse a couple of times to memorize before going home.

notes

Have the courage to stand firm

Biblical References: Daniel 3; 6; Hebrews 11:32-12:3.

Lesson Objective: That preteens learn that having faith in God gives us courage.

Memory Verse: *Therefore, since we are surrounded by such a great cloud of witnesses, let us throw off everything that hinders and the sin that so easily entangles. And let us run with perseverance the race marked out for us* (Hebrews 12:1).

PREPARE YOURSELF TO TEACH!

It is difficult for the preteen to express and defend his faith when his Christian friends are not around to support him. It is often easier for him to give in to pressure than to defend his beliefs.

Perhaps he has a sincere desire to please God, but he does not know what to do when others insist on keeping him away from his convictions. Only a solid faith in God will give him the courage to resist the pressure.

The lives of Daniel, Azariah, Mishael and Ananias will be models of faith and courage for them. These young people did not abandon their relationship with God, even when their life was in danger.

Through this lesson, preteens will learn that the courage to defend our relationship with God is born of faith in him. Just as Daniel's faith served as a testimony for others, the lives of your students will be a living testimony to their friends. Their reaction to pressures and problems will impact them, and it will make a difference in their personal testimony.

BIBLICAL COMMENTARY

Daniel 3. In this chapter, we read how the faith of Ananias, Mishael and Azariah was tested. King Nebuchadnezzar had built a huge golden statue and those who refused to worship it would die in the furnace of fire.

The three young men refused to betray God by worshiping the image, since by doing so they would not only have broken the commandments, but would have destroyed their relationship with God.

When the king questioned them, they did not deny the charges; rather they affirmed their faith that God could save them from the fire. However, their faith was not based on the fact that God could deliver them. They told the king that, even if God did not save them, they would not worship the statue.

When God saved them from the fire, Nebuchadnezzar recognized the greatness of the Lord of Israel. After asking them to come out of the furnace, he ordered that no one speak against their God because He was truly powerful.

Daniel 6. Daniel's faith faced a similar test under the command of the Median king Darius. The other officers of the kingdom were jealous because Daniel, despite being a Hebrew, was the second most important man in the kingdom.

The officers proposed that for 30 days, no one should be worshiped except the king, and whoever did otherwise would be thrown into the lions' den. Thinking that Daniel had approved that law, the king signed it.

Since Daniel did not stop praying to God, the officers denounced him. The king, who could not revoke the law, with much regret watched while the guards threw Daniel into the pit of lions. The next day the king went to the pit, and found Daniel alive.

He gave honor to God for having delivered Daniel. Then the king recognized the God of Daniel as the only living, eternal and powerful God, and declared that all should fear and revere Him. As further proof that God had intervened, the lions devoured those who had conspired against Daniel.

DEVELOPMENT OF THE LESSON

I would do anything for ...!

Have the students turn to page 175 of their worksheets, and ask them to complete the sentence on the indicated line. Then, guide your students in a game to guess the answers of their classmates.

Ask for some volunteers to ask questions of others, trying to find out what they wrote. For example: Is it an object? It's an animal? Is it something you can buy? Can you get it in a store? Is it colored? Can you carry it in your arms? If the answer to each question is "yes", the volunteer will continue to ask until they receive a "no" answer. There they must give a turn to another person and so on until someone guesses what the person wrote.

BIBLE STORY

During the week, read the Bible story of Daniel 3, and think about how you would relate it in your own words. Remember that you need to become very familiar with the lesson in order to tell a good story.

The statue that King Nebuchadnezzar made was about thirty meters high and three meters wide. It was a gigantic monument, because the king wanted it to be seen from everywhere in the kingdom.

After telling the rest of the biblical story, ask your students: What do you think about what the Hebrew youth told the king, even knowing they could be thrown into the fiery furnace? They trusted God with all their being, not only because they believed that God could deliver them, but because they wanted to please Him, even if it meant dying for their beliefs.

Daniel faced another dangerous situation when he was locked in a den with lions.

Persecution

Talk about the value that these four friends showed when facing death in a strange country where other gods were worshiped. Emphasize that it would have been very easy for them to give in to the pressure of others, but they did not.

Ask your class to read Hebrews 11:32-12:3, and answer the questions on page 176 of their worksheets.

1. Who are some of the Old Testament heroes mentioned because of their faith?
2. According to verses 36-38, what types of persecution did they face?
3. In Hebrews 12:1, what does the writer compare to the Christian life?
4. According to Hebrews 12:2, how is Jesus a model for us?
5. In Hebrews 12:3, how does Jesus help those who are facing persecution today?
6. In what ways are Christians persecuted today?
7. How can Christians have the courage to stand firm despite persecution?

TO FINISH

You learned?

You will need cards to write each of the following questions separately. Each student should take a card, read the question and answer it.

1. The young Hebrews learned that they could stand firm in their religious beliefs. What did you learn?
2. Daniel helped the king understand the meaning of his dream. What did you learn?
3. Daniel helped Belshazzar understand the meaning of the writing on the wall. What did you learn?
4. Daniel learned to trust in God when he was in the lions' den. What did you learn?
5. What did you learn about God in this series of lessons?
6. What did you learn about yourself in these lessons?

Finally, form a circle and ask everyone to pray silently for the person on their right. Finish praying for each of your students. Ask God to help you all during the week that begins and not forget to intercede for the brothers and sisters who suffer persecution around the world.

CHRISTMAS PROMISES

Biblical basis: Genesis 12:1-3; Deuteronomy 7:9; 2 Samuel 7:12-13; Psalm 31:14-15; Isaiah 7:14; 11:1; Jeremiah 33:12-15; Micah 5:2; Matthew 1:1, 6, 18-25; 2:1-23; Luke 1:26-38; 2:1-7, 8-20; John 4:42; 14:1-3.

Unit verse: *This is how God showed his love among us: He sent his one and only Son into the world that we might live through him. This is love: not that we loved God, but that he loved us and sent his Son as an atoning sacrifice for our sins* (1 John 4:9-10).

Purposes of the unit

This unit will help preteens to:

- Understand that the birth of Jesus was the fulfillment of the Old Testament prophecies.
- Recognize the importance of knowing Jesus personally as Savior and Lord.
- Trust that God always keeps his promises.
- Tell others the good news of the birth of Jesus.

Lessons from the unit

Lesson 49: Good News

Lesson 50: It was worth the wait!

Lesson 51: How the Good News is given

Lesson 52: A long trip to see a king

Lesson 53: Review of Unit XI

Why do pre-teens need the teaching of this unit?

Christmas is the most celebrated holiday in the whole world. Some preteens may have lost the enthusiasm they felt for this celebration when they were younger, but they still look forward to it.

They know the story of Christmas, but for many, it is only a story. The most exciting things are the gifts and the delicious food. The biblical stories of this unit will serve to reflect on the true meaning of Christmas, helping them to recognize the importance of knowing personally the true reason for Christmas: Jesus.

They will study the birth of Christ from a new perspective: learning that God planned that birth long before it happened. They will discover the joy that surrounded the birth of the Savior and the emotion that compelled the shepherds to tell everyone the news.

Through these lessons, your students will learn that God keeps His promises. And, although it is sometimes difficult to wait for God's answer, they will know that no matter how much time they must wait, they can trust God because He always remains faithful.

It is our desire that during this Christmas season, you and your class will take time to meditate on the love of God, which manifested itself by sending Jesus to earth as a sacrifice for our sins. Talk with your students about the joy of knowing that we have a faithful God who has provided for us the path to eternal life.

Good News

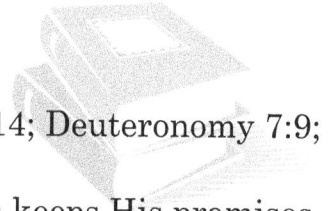

Biblical References: Matthew 1:18-25; Luke 1:26-38; Isaiah 7:14; Deuteronomy 7:9; John 14:1-3.

Lesson Objective: That preteens learn to trust God who always keeps His promises.

Memory Verse: *This is how God showed his love among us: He sent his one and only Son into the world that we might live through him. This is love: not that we loved God, but that he loved us and sent his Son as an atoning sacrifice for our sins* (1 John 4:9-10).

PREPARE YOURSELF TO TEACH!

During this stage of their growth, preadolescents are rapidly developing the ability to reason, and begin to understand the complex relationship between ideas and facts. They have the ability to understand that the birth of Jesus is more than a holiday or a miraculous event. This lesson will help them know that the birth of Jesus was part of God's plan from the beginning of mankind. For hundreds of years, God had promised to send a Savior, and that promise was fulfilled with the birth of Christ.

Perhaps your students are disappointed in their friends and family members who make promises and do not keep them, but in this biblical story, they will learn to trust that God is faithful. Even if others fail you, you can trust that God will keep his promises. He may not respond instantly or when you want it; however, he always has the right answer at the right time.

BIBLICAL COMMENTARY

Matthew 1:18-25; Luke 1:26-38; Isaiah 7:14; Deuteronomy 7:9; John 14:1-3. The prophets of the Old Testament announced the arrival of a promised Messiah. Actually, the whole Old Testament refers to his coming. Isaiah, Jeremiah, Micah and other prophets gave specific details about the circumstances in which the new King would be born. And all those prophecies were fulfilled with the birth of Jesus.

Today's biblical story is about the announcement of that birth. When the angel Gabriel told Mary that she would be the mother of the Messiah, she was confused. "How can I be a mother being a virgin?" She asked herself. But the angel assured her, "Nothing is impossible for God" (Luke 1:37). It is likely that she recalled the prophecy of Isaiah 7:14, where the prophet affirmed that the mother of the Messiah would be a virgin.

Although this would possibly ruin her marriage plans, and cause serious problems in Jewish society, Mary trusted in God and submitted to his will.

When Joseph found out that Mary was pregnant, he did not know what to do. They were engaged, but Joseph knew that he was not the father of the child. By law, he could have demanded that they punish Mary for committing adultery. But because he loved her, he was considering leaving her in secret.

However, God sent an angel to tell Joseph to continue with the marriage plans, because he had chosen Mary to be the mother of the Messiah.

Thus the prophecy of Isaiah was fulfilled, demonstrating that God is faithful to his word and worthy of all our trust.

DEVELOPMENT OF THE LESSON

A baby!

Divide the class into small groups. Provide newspapers, tape and some towels or fabrics. Ask them to make a paper baby with the newspaper, and wrap it in the cloth. Next, allow each group to show the finished baby.

Then, tell them: For many it is difficult to wait patiently for the arrival of a baby. How many of you have a younger brother or sister? How did they feel while you waited for him to be born? Were you excited?

In today's lesson we will study the announcement of the birth of a very special baby, which many people waited for for hundreds of years.

How long did the people wait?

Ask for two volunteers to help you hand out the student worksheets. Then, have them go to page 178.

Ask your students to look at the illustrations. Next, request that three or four read the text aloud, while you write some key words on the board (eg, creation, Noah, Abraham, Moses, Passover, Ten Commandments, prophets, exile).

Tell them: As we have read, through the history of the Hebrew people, God showed his faithfulness and promised to send a Messiah to save mankind from their sins. These promises came true with the birth of Jesus in Bethlehem.

Why did God wait so long?

Read together the information found on page 179 of the student worksheets. Have some volunteers read certain paragraphs of the text. Explain the difficult concepts, and make sure everyone understands the complete information.

Emphasize that, although we do not know why God chose to send Jesus at that moment in history, we do not doubt his wisdom in choosing the perfect time.

BIBLE STORY

Let the preteens sit in a circle, and ask them: Have you ever waited for something with a lot of expectation? How did you feel when you saw that time had passed and what you hoped for did not arrive?

Listen to their responses and tell them how the Israelites felt as they awaited the arrival of the Messiah.

Since this biblical story is well known, we suggest that, based on the biblical passage of study, you tell it with your own words. You could start it in the following way:

For hundreds of years, the prophets, who were messengers of God, spoke about the Messiah who would come to save the people from their sins. Isaiah wrote one of those prophecies.

Ask a volunteer to read Isaiah 7:14.

Continue telling the story of the announcement of Jesus' birth, and at the appropriate time, ask someone else to read the angel's message to Joseph in Matthew 1:20-21.

ACTIVITIES

The wait was almost over when ...

Have the students find page 179 of the worksheet to review the lesson using the phrases that appear there. Ask them that, after reading the expressions that are inside the squares, mark with an X those that are false and with an O that are true. Then, think about what they should change in the false sentences to make it true. Use these answers to check what your students answered:

- Mary and Joseph were already married. (X) False - They were engaged to get married.
- The angel Gabriel told Mary that she would have a baby. (O) True.
- The angel Gabriel told Mary that the child would be called Joseph. (X) False - The baby was to be called Jesus.
- The power of the Holy Spirit helped Mary to get pregnant with the baby Jesus, even though she was a virgin. (O) True.
- Joseph was glad when he learned that Mary was pregnant. (O) False - Joseph was saddened.
- Joseph planned to divorce Mary. (O) True.
- An angel told Joseph to take Mary as his wife. (O) True.

- The angel told Joseph that the baby's name would be Jesus. (O) True.

- After this, Joseph and Mary got married. (O) True.

Broken promises

Ask the class: Has it ever happen to you that a person did not keep a promise that he or she made to you? Maybe you got angry, cried or lost confidence in that person. Why do you think it is important that we keep our promises?

Read Deuteronomy 7:9. How many generations does the Bible say that God keeps his promises? (For a thousand generations). That means that God will always be faithful to us.

Do you think it was right that the people of God waited so long for the arrival of Jesus? In fact, many people had lost hope and no longer believed in the arrival of the Messiah, because they thought he had waited a long time.

Emphasize the phrase "Jehovah your God is God" to tell them that we should trust in His faithfulness, even if it seems that we have waited a long time for Him to fulfill His promises.

Write a poem

To do the activity on page 180 of the worksheet, your preteens should write a line of five lines that do not rhyme, following these instructions:

- Line 1: subject;
- Line 2: two adjectives that describe the subject;
- Line 3: two verbs or actions performed by the subject;
- Line 4: a six-word comment on the subject;
- Line 5: a word that is synonymous with the subject.

Observe the example in the student worksheet, and give them time to develop a verse without rhyme for Mary and another for Joseph.

TO FINISH

Explain to the preteens that we Christians have waited for the second coming of Jesus for hundreds of years, but he has not returned yet. However, God will be faithful to keep his promise, just as he did when he sent his Son the first time.

Finally, ask them: Are you ready for the second coming of Christ?

Challenge your students to tell some people during the week that God keeps his promises. Encourage them to take time to thank God for all the promises he has kept in their lives.

Review the Memory verse. Then, invite them to the next class to continue the theme of the birth of Jesus.

notes

It was worth the wait!

Biblical References: Genesis 12:1-3; 2 Samuel 7:12-13; Psalm 31:14-15a; Matthew 1:1; Luke 2:1-7.

Lesson Objective: That the students trust God with their future.

Memory Verse: *This is how God showed his love among us: He sent his one and only Son into the world that we might live through him. This is love: not that we loved God, but that he loved us and sent his Son as an atoning sacrifice for our sins* (1 John 4:9-10).

PREPARE YOURSELF TO TEACH!

For preteens, waiting patiently is a difficult thing to do. They struggle between "I want it now" (the typical attitude of preadolescents), and "I can wait" (patience that is obtained with maturity).

Your students are in a stage in which they face great changes. On the one hand, they want to be teenagers and enjoy the privileges of that age; and, on the other, they still enjoy the activities of childhood. However, the most important thing is that they learn to enjoy every moment of their lives, waiting patiently for the events that will come later.

Adults who love children and fear teens often overlook preadolescents. For that reason, your students need to know that they are important to God, that he works in their lives, and that this age is part of God's plan for them.

BIBLICAL COMMENTARY

Genesis 12:1-3; 2 Samuel 7:12-13; Matthew 1:1. God made a special promise to Abraham: that his descendants would be a blessing to the whole earth. And to David He promised He would establish his throne forever. These promises surely seemed uncertain. However, God does everything in the perfect time, and fulfilled both promises in Christ.

God sent Jesus at the opportune time, when world conditions were appropriate to proclaim the gospel. It is true that the Jews were under the rule of Rome, but that situation provided a universal language and a period of relative peace. These factors facilitated the spread of the gospel by land and sea. When was Jesus born? We do not know the exact date, but we know the purpose, the promise and the fulfillment of his coming.

Luke 2:1-7. God used the census ordered by Augustus Caesar for Mary and Joseph to travel to Bethlehem, fulfilling the prophecy of Micah 5:2. "Bethlehem" in Hebrew means "house of bread", and from that house came Jesus, the bread of life.

The census for which Mary and Joseph went to Bethlehem had several purposes. The main one was the collection of taxes. Being a descendant of David, Joseph had to go to the city of David to register. The journey of more than 149 kilometers lasted perhaps four days. Maria did not need to register, but perhaps she preferred to accompany Joseph on that exhausting trip, instead of staying in town and listening to the gossip about her unusual pregnancy.

Therefore, Jesus was born in Bethlehem, but not in an inn, but probably in a cave. In that region there are many caves where the shepherds and their animals used to take refuge when they went to Bethlehem. The manger was perhaps carved in stone to prevent the animals from overturning it. If the stable was a cave, the circumstances of Jesus' birth were similar to those of his burial. Both events took place in borrowed caves, and in the fulfillment of the time established by God.

DEVELOPMENT OF THE LESSON

What do you care about?

Write the word "CONCERN" in large letters on the board. Ask your students to help you create a list of concerns they have about their future (for example: studies, family problems, friends, illnesses, etc.).

Then, ask them: How do you feel when you think about the future? Are you worried about what your life will be like when you are 18 or 21?

Last week we talked about Mary and Joseph. Their lives changed radically after receiving the angel's visit and knowing that they would have a baby. Do you think they were worried about their future? Why?

Listen to their answers, and tell them that in today's story they will learn not to worry about the coming events.

BIBLE STORY

Tell the story of Jesus' birth in your own words, using the following story as a guide:

Thousands of years before Jesus was born, God asked Abraham to leave his country to go to a new land. He had promised that his descendants would become a great nation and that through them, He would bless all the families of the earth (read Genesis 12:1-3).

One of Abraham's descendants was David. God also made a promise to David; He told him that through his descendants, his kingdom would never end (read Samuel 7:12-13).

Look up Matthew 1:1 and 1:17. What do these verses tell us about the fulfillment of God's promise to Abraham and David? Allow your students to respond (Jesus was a descendant of Abraham and David).

Tell the story, and conclude by saying: God fulfilled His promises to Abraham and David. The birth of Jesus was part of God's plan to send a Savior, and He worked in the lives of many people to fulfill that plan. It was not luck or coincidence. God planned everything very carefully.

Joseph and Mary were perhaps worried about their future. Their plans for courtship and wedding changed with the news of the birth of a very special baby. They could have let themselves be overcome by panic, despair and seek their own solution. However, God was working with that couple and others for Jesus to be born in Bethlehem.

Part of the plan

God worked in many people to fulfill the plan of salvation. To deepen this concept, ask your students to solve the riddles on page 181 of their worksheets. Use this guide to verify that their answers are correct:

- I had faith and followed God wherever he guided me. I was an ancestor of Jesus. (Abraham)
- I was a shepherd and a king. I was an ancestor of Jesus. (David)
- An angel told me that I would be the mother of Jesus. (Mary)

- God used the decree that I gave to take a national census. My decree led Joseph and Mary to Bethlehem. (Augustus Cesar)
- God gave me courage to overcome doubts and cultural traditions. I married a young woman who was pregnant. (Joseph)

The news of Bethlehem

The Jews had waited many years for the arrival of the new king. Galatians 4:4 tells us, "But when the set time had fully come, God sent his Son ..." What does that mean? Help the preteens to understand that God had designed a special plan, according to which he sent Jesus at the right time. Then ask them: What kind of celebration would they expect for the birth of a king? Where do you think would be the best place for a king to be born? How should newborns be treated? Why did God choose to bring his Son into the world in this way?

Read together the "news of Bethlehem" on pages 182 and 183 of the student worksheet. Then, talk about how you imagine that it was on the night of Jesus' birth.

Patience please!

Give a short testimony about how God worked in your personal life. Help your students understand that God wants to work in all areas of one's life, because he is interested in us and wants everyone to enjoy a full and abundant life. That does not mean that everything will always be as we wish. Many times we will have to learn to be patient and wait for God's response.

Have the kids go to page 184 of their worksheets. Give them time to read the letters and respond to them, encouraging them to patiently wait for God's work.

TO FINISH

Review the list of concerns your students wrote at the beginning of the class. Then, read together Matthew 1:20 and Luke 1:30, and ask them: What is the phrase that is repeated in both passages? (Do not be afraid.)

Remind them that they should not fear what comes in the future if they have the presence of God in their life. Guide them in a time of prayer, asking God to help them increase their patience and their faith.

How the Good News is given

Biblical References: Isaiah 11:1; Jeremiah 33:12-15; Matthew 1:6; Luke 2:8-20.

Lesson Objective: That the preteens learn to tell others about the joy they feel about the birth of Jesus.

Memory Verse: *This is how God showed his love among us: He sent his one and only Son into the world that we might live through him. This is love: not that we loved God, but that he loved us and sent his Son as an atoning sacrifice for our sins (1 John 4:9-10).*

PREPARE YOURSELF TO TEACH!

Perhaps your students have accepted Jesus Christ as their Savior and Lord, but only some speak with others about their faith. Maybe they do not know how to witness or, as time has gone by, they've lost the emotion they felt in surrendering to Christ.

This lesson will help your class understand that the birth of Jesus is a cause for celebration, and that witnessing about it does not always mean explaining the plan of salvation. As in the case of pastors, our testimony will be very effective if we tell others about the joy that Jesus gives us. Encourage your students to learn to tell others the good news of Jesus' birth, and to reflect in their lives the joy of personally knowing the Savior and Lord.

BIBLICAL COMMENTARY

Isaiah 11:1; Jeremiah 33:12-15; Matthew 1:6; Luke 2:8-20. Jesus was born in a manger, not by accident, but because it was part of God's plan. The first to receive the good news were the shepherds, while they tended their sheep in the field during the night. Furthermore, in Isaiah 11:1 it was prophesied that the Messiah would descend from the line of Jesse, David's father. Since David had been a shepherd, it was appropriate that the first to hear the glorious news about the birth of Jesus were shepherds.

The angels gave the news of the birth of the Messiah to humble shepherds, not to rulers or religious leaders. That fact was very significant, because it was to common and hardworking people. Religious leaders despised shepherds for not keeping the Sabbath, and under the law of Moses, many Jews considered them impure. Jesus himself was accused of violating the Sabbath and being impure by associating with people that society rejected.

The announcement to the shepherds also showed that Christ came first to the Jews. They awaited the Messiah, and God honored them for believing in His promises.

The shepherds, feeling the need to go to Bethlehem, left their work to seek the Savior and worship Him.

Through this passage we can know the joy that must have filled their hearts. After worshiping the newborn King, the shepherds returned to their work. They praised God and told the news to everyone they met on their way. Their hearts overflowed with joy after coming face to face with the Savior.

Do we feel that same joy and transmit it to others? If we show the joy we have in Christ, as the shepherds did many years ago, people will know the love of God, seeing it reflected in us.

DEVELOPMENT OF THE LESSON

After welcoming your students and praying to start the class, talk about how difficult it is to wait for Christmas. Many pre-teens anxiously await this special day and count the days until the celebration. However, in the previous lesson we learned that we must wait patiently, not only for important dates, but for God's work in our lives.

News, news!

For this activity you will need a daily newspaper and figures of a radio, a television and a computer.

Show the images to your students, and ask them what they all have in common. Listen to their answers and, based on them, explain that these objects represent the media or information. Through them we learn about the news that happens around us and around the world.

Divide the class into groups of three or four students. Deliver one sheet of newspaper to each group, and ask them to find good news and cut it out.

Then tell them that today's story tells us about some men who proclaimed good news.

Guess what happened!

Guide the students' attention to page 185 of their worksheets. Ask them to complete the sentences about the most exciting experiences they have had.

Then, ask them: What do people do when they are excited about good news? (They want to tell it.) If you had exciting news, who would you like to tell?

In today's story, we will hear about some people who received very exciting news, and we will see what they did.

BIBLE STORY

Read the study passages in advance and tell the shepherds' story following this text as a guide.

What do they do when they can not sleep? Allow a storm of ideas until someone mentions that the solution is to count sheep. Then, tell them: Imagine what it would be like to count sheep for life. Boring? Tiring? Would they lose count?

It all started on a quiet night, while a group of shepherds cared for their sheep. Nothing exciting happened on that side of the mountain. Maybe sometimes the shepherds wanted a wild animal to appear to stop the boredom. Suddenly, the darkness was gone and the sky was filled with radiance. It was an angel! The shepherds were frightened, but the angel told them ... (in advance ask someone to read Luke 2:10-12 at that time).

Then, more angels appeared singing praises to God (ask another student to read Luke 2:14).

It seemed that the earth trembled! Or maybe it was the shepherds who trembled with fear? When the angels disappeared, the shepherds were so excited they said ... (Read all together Luke 2:15). Maybe they did something they had never done before: they left their sheep and ran to Bethlehem.

There they found Joseph, Mary and baby Jesus. After worshiping Jesus, the shepherds returned to watch over their flocks; they praised God and told everyone what they had seen and heard.

Proclaim the good news

Have them find page 186 in their worksheets. Then, read Luke 2:16-18 and ask your class to write in their own words what they believe the shepherds told people about the angels' message and Jesus' birth.

To announce!

Tell your students: God wants us to express our joy for the birth of Jesus to others. Then, write on the board: "Tell others about Jesus." Talk about the meaning of each word. What should we tell about Jesus? How can we talk about Jesus if others do not want to listen? To whom should we tell the good news? Write your students' answers on the board. Emphasize that today, most people live in a hurry and it is often difficult to get them to stop to listen to the Word of God. We need to be prepared to talk to people about Jesus and be precise in our message.

Have the kids look up page 187 of the students' worksheets and do the suggested activity. They will need time to write simple poems of two lines that express the truth about Jesus and the joy of knowing him. Read the examples on the worksheet and allow them to work together to write their poems.

How will I tell them?

Turn the page and, in conclusion, read together Psalm 96:3. Then, have the students write some ideas about how they can announce to others the good news of the birth of Jesus (for example: invite friends to the Bible class, give testimony through good behavior, visit the sick, help those in need, etc.). Then, read the lists aloud to exchange ideas.

TO FINISH

Intercede in prayer for the people your students will share the Good News with during this week.

Say goodbye by singing a Christmas song, and do not forget to invite them to the next class.

A long trip to see a king

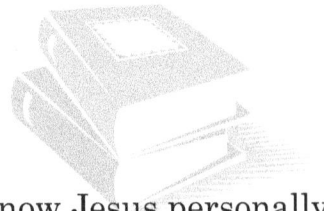

Biblical References: Micah 5:2; Matthew 2:1-23; John 4:42.

Lesson Objective: That pre-teens recognize that they need to know Jesus personally.

Memory Verse: *This is how God showed his love among us: He sent his one and only Son into the world that we might live through him. This is love: not that we loved God, but that he loved us and sent his Son as an atoning sacrifice for our sins (1 John 4:9-10).*

PREPARE YOURSELF TO TEACH!

Pre-teens are developing the ability to make decisions and carry out those decisions. Some have already accepted Christ as their Savior and Lord, but they think that this is the end of everything. They need to understand that being a Christian is not an act, but a relationship; it is a lifelong commitment to Jesus Christ and his teachings. This lesson will motivate them to grow in their personal relationship with Jesus, helping them to renew their commitment to live for him.

Some pre-teens may have heard the stories and teachings about Jesus for a long time, but never accepted him as Savior and Lord. Maybe they think they are Christians, but they do not understand what that means. This lesson will clarify the difference between knowing about God and knowing Him personally.

BIBLICAL COMMENTARY

Micah 5:2; Matthew 2:1-23. The wise men of the east present a great contrast in the history of Christmas. Their wealth and social position stood out on the humble stage of Bethlehem, in contrast to the condition of Mary, Joseph and the shepherds. These powerful men, with great academic training, advised kings, studied the stars and interpreted dreams.

Their nationality and religion were different from the inhabitants of Bethlehem. They came from the east, perhaps from Persia, and perhaps they did not practice the Jewish religion. However, they had heard the prophecies about the promised Messiah, and they feared God.

The visit of the sages shows the inclusive nature of the gospel. Jesus came for all people: Jews and Gentiles. The Good News is for everyone.

A star motivated the wise to start their journey and guided them every day on their journey. How appropriate it was to be guided by a star! The stars shine more in the dark, because they are seen more clearly. The wise sought the truth and found Jesus, the "shining star of the morning" and the source of all truth.

John 4:42. The Gospel of John tells us about another group of men who sought Jesus. After hearing the testimony of the Samaritan woman, they wanted to know more about him, and they were not disappointed. That's why they told the woman, "We no longer believe only because of your saying, but because we ourselves have heard, and we know that this is truly the Savior of the world, the Christ."

DEVELOPMENT OF THE LESSON

Verses on the wall

This activity will serve as a review of the memory verse. Write each phrase of 1 John 4:9-10 on a different piece of paper. Place them in disorder on a wall of the classroom. Ask your students to place the phrases in the correct order and read them in the right way.

What is myrrh?

Ask two volunteers to help you hand out the student worksheets and have them all find page 189 and read the definition of "myrrh".

Then, they are to look in their Bibles for the texts suggested in the concordance, so that they understand the meaning of this gift that the wise men brought to Jesus, and answer the following questions:

- Who brought myrrh to the baby Jesus? (Matthew 2:11 - The wise brought him gold, incense and myrrh).

- How was myrrh offered to Jesus on the cross? (Mark 15:23 - The soldiers offered him wine mixed with myrrh to alleviate his pain, but Jesus rejected him).

- For what did Nicodemus use myrrh after Jesus died? (John 19:39-40 - Nicodemus took myrrh, oil and spices to anoint the body of Jesus).

Famous characters

Ask your students to name famous people they admire, and say why.

Then ask them: How do they know all that about those people? Did you meet some of them in person? Did you get their autograph or have a picture taken with any of them?

Explain that even if we know certain facts about a celebrity, that does not mean that we really know them, unless we have spent time with that person.

Today's story tells us about some very important men who knew some facts about the baby Jesus, but wanted to investigate to get to know him personally.

BIBLE STORY

For this activity, assign several students to look up Matthew 2:2, 8, 13-18 and Micah 5:2. Ask them to read their verse when you tell them, as you tell the Bible story. Remember that it is important that you read the study passage in advance, so that you are familiar with the details and are ready to answer any questions.

If you have visual material to illustrate your lesson, it would be very helpful.

More than a name

Say to the class: The wise men traveled to Bethlehem to see Jesus. When they arrived, they knelt down and worshiped him. They had some information about Jesus, but that was not enough; they wanted to meet him.

Ask them to go to page 190 of their worksheets, and using the letters of the name JESUS, make an acrostic with the data they know about him. For example:

Just
Emanuel, God with us
Savior
Unconditional love
Son of God

After this exercise, instruct them to use the letters of their respective names to make an acrostic that suggests ways they can learn more about Jesus.

A gift for the King

Hand out white paper and colored pencils for your students to draw the gift they would like to give Jesus. Let each decide what to draw, and then pass it on to the group. Remember that all the contributions of your students are important. Stay alert to avoid negative comments about a classmate's work.

Then, ask the preteens to describe their drawing, and stick them on a poster board to create a wall mural, which they will title "My Gift to Jesus."

TO FINISH

Sing some Christmas songs, and form a prayer circle to thank God for his love and for his Son Jesus, our Savior, and intercede for the group's requests.

Before saying goodbye, emphasize that the best gift Jesus desires from us is our faith and obedience. Encourage your students to spend time with the Lord during the week to get to know Him better.

Remind them that the next class will be the last of the year, and therefore, their attendance is very important.

Lesson 53

Review of Unit XI - A story without end

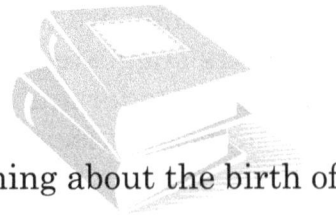

Lesson Objective: That the preadolescents reinforce their learning about the birth of Christ and joyfully celebrate his birth.

Memory Verse: *This is how God showed his love among us: He sent his one and only Son into the world that we might live through him. This is love: not that we loved God, but that he loved us and sent his Son as an atoning sacrifice for our sins (1 John 4:9-10).*

PREPARE YOURSELF TO TEACH!

It has been 52 Sundays since you began this cycle of teaching with your students. Remember the first day? The new and shiny book, full of fascinating stories to study. However, now the passage of time has left a mark on your book; but above all, it has left an indelible mark on the hearts of your students.

We suggest you use this lesson to review some of the stories you covered in this unit, and also to celebrate the year of work that is about to conclude.

Pre-teens enjoy fellowship, especially when it comes to celebrating special dates, such as the arrival of a new year. Take this opportunity to enjoy Christian love with your students and let them feel your appreciation.

Because it is the last class of the year, it is a good opportunity to reflect on how your teaching has impacted your preadolescents. Do you see the spiritual growth of your students? Do you notice a more mature attitude in them? Did they develop the habit of prayer and reading the Word?

Remember that a teacher's task never ends, especially when it comes to Christian teachers. We do not just cultivate knowledge in the mind, but we sow the Word of God in their hearts. Therefore, our responsibility is to pray and ensure that this seed grows and bears fruit in abundance. It is our desire and prayer that in this year that is ending, that God will bless your ministry and enable you to accomplish the task to which he called you.

DEVELOPMENT OF THE LESSON

Have your students sit in a circle, and ask them why they think today's lesson is titled "A story without end ..."

Listen carefully to their answers, and explain that the Christmas story did not end with the birth of Christ, because it was a fact that impacted the history of humanity and brought with it eternal consequences.

When Christ came to earth and died on the cross, he completed the plan of salvation that God had designed to free mankind from a terrible eternal destiny, opening the door for us to attain eternal life. That means that the story of God's love for his children will never end, because we will live with him for ever and ever in heavenly mansions.

Review of the unit

Have your students find page 192 of their worksheets. Divide the class into small groups to do the activity together.

Tell them how to assemble the game board by placing a clip in the center of the circle and inserting the tip of a pencil in the center, so that the clip does not move from its place when it is spun around. Each participant will spin the clip and answer the question it stops on, using what they have learned from the previous lessons.

Jesus, my personal Savior

Guide your students to a time of reflection, and ask how many of them accepted Christ in their hearts.

Use the steps on page 191 of the student's book to explain the plan of salvation to preteens, and invite them to receive Christ as their personal Savior. Then, address in prayer those who have decided to accept the invitation.

Remind them that although many people can read the Bible and know some facts about Jesus, the most important thing is to have him as a friend and Lord of your life.

Encourage them to develop a personal relationship with Jesus. To do this, they should read a passage of the Bible every day, and spend time in prayer and communion with Jesus' during the week.

Celebration time!

After the teaching time, we suggest that you enjoy a time of celebration with your students, thanking God for the teachings of the year that's ending, celebrating the birth of Jesus and the arrival of a new year.

Decorate the room with colored papers.

Organize some group games, and if possible, prepare a simple snack. Here we suggest three simple and economical recipes.

Rice with milk and apples
Ingredients:
1/2 cup of milk
2 cups cooked rice
1 apple cut into cubes.
2 tablespoons of brown sugar
1 pinch of cinnamon
1 teaspoon of honey
1 cup of any fruit

Preparation:

Heat the milk in a saucepan until just before it boils. Add the other ingredients, stir and bring to medium heat for ten minutes. Garnish with the fruit.

Sugar cookies
Ingredients:
1 cup of butter (butter)
1 cup of sugar.
2 eggs (separate the whites from the yolks)
2 cups of common flour.
2 teaspoons of baking powder.
1 teaspoon salt.
1 spoonful of milk
1 Teaspoon vanilla extract.

Preparation:

Whip the butter until it is creamy. Add the sugar and the yolks. Sift together the flour, baking powder and salt. Join with the butter mixture. Beat the whites until they are firm and incorporate them into the dough. Add milk and vanilla. Stretch and roll out the dough and cut with molds in the desired shape. Sprinkle with sugar and bake at 350 degrees F (180 degrees C) in a preheated oven.

Strawberry Triangles

Ingredients:

4 slices of wheat bread.

1 cup of strawberries

3 tablespoons of strawberry sweet jam or jelly.

Preparation:

Trim the bread crust. Wash the strawberries very well and make them puree. Spread one side of the bread with the strawberry puree, and bend the edges of the loaves to form triangles. Then seal the edges with the strawberries. Bake five minutes.

TO FINISH

Thank your students for attending classes throughout the year.

Distribute all the work they have done throughout the year.

Take a few minutes to pray for each of your students and ask God to continue to help them grow in their spiritual lives.

Say goodbye affectionately.

Christian education material for children

Mesoamerica Region Discipleship Ministries presents with satisfaction its complete collection of Christian education books.

They were designed for teachers of children and for students from 4 to 11 years of age.

Children will learn the lessons of the Bible according to their age. And, by the end of their elementary school years, they will have gone through the challenging biblical stories, as well as various topics appropriate to each stage of their childhood and pre-adolescence.

This material was designed as different steps to achieve a holy life. It contains clear and possible goals.

The teacher's book will help equip those who have the beautiful task of leading children to connect with the message that will change their lives forever.

By promoting the child to the next year-according to his age-he will have studied only once each of the books. When he reaches 12 years of age - if he started with the first book - he will have studied the eight books of this valuable collection.

The books are designed to be used in Sunday school classes, happy hours, Saturday Bible schools, children's clubs, discipleship classes, and schools in general.

This series aims to:
a. Challenge the children to learn the Word of God.
b. Encourage them to grow in their Christian experience as children of God.
c. Guide them to accept Jesus as their savior and Lord.
d. Help them grow in their faith
e. Help them become part of the faith community, the church.

The following table will help you identify the corresponding book according to the age of the students:

- Preschoolers: 4 and 5 years old (Year / book 1 and 2).

- Elementary: 6, 7, 8 years of age (Year / book 1, 2 and 3).

- Words of Life (preadolescents): 9, 10, 11 years of age (Year / book 1, 2 and 3).

www.ingramcontent.com/pod-product-compliance
Lightning Source LLC
Chambersburg PA
CBHW081541040426
42448CB00015B/3172